'I AM I'
ANGELIC
MESSAGES
ORACLE BOOK

STEPHANIE J. KING

AUTHOR | SPEAKER | SOULPRENUER™

Published by
Filament Publishing Ltd
16, Croydon Road, Waddon, Croydon,
Surrey, CR0 4PA, United Kingdom
Telephone +44 (0)20 8688 2598
Fax +44 (0)20 7183 7186
info@filamentpublishing.com
www.filamentpublishing.com

ISBN 978-1-913192-33-4

Printed by IngramSpark

Dedication

To those living, to those passed, to those still yet to come...

To those awake and those asleep but yet to stir...

To those who shine their light and to those who will shine brighter...

To those in service in this world...

To all those who wish to be loved and happy; to end Karma and old programming cycles...

You are love unconditional yourself.

You are precisely where you should be at this moment in time – to step forward towards levels NOW emerging.

You have birthed many times to get to this point.

'Happy Ever After' is beckoning, in view and in reach.

Through free will and choice, the rest remains firmly with you...

To my children... to my parents... to my family...

(I am I) When you walk in union with Me – you will not fear or be worried again – for you are protected by our very alignment, you are cocooned in the energy of My presence. When you walk in truth, in innocence and love – no harm can befall you. When you triumph over Karma, over cause and effect, when your first and last thoughts are 'how may I serve?' you walk with the highest that also serve Me, you work in the name of the One. (I am I)

Author's note

This work is a three-way link between yourself, your angels/ guardian and God.

Any reference to 'man' in this book is the Universal word for humanity, for mankind as a whole. It is not intended to place the male gender over or above the female. All are equal.

All writing by **'I am I'** is channelled directly from God – from the Universal/Earth/Mind energy source. All speak directly with you.

For more information visit **www.stephaniejking.com**

Testimonial

"How truth can help you – I know well myself. Free of illusion and ego – this book is a true inspiration that will heighten your awareness and purpose to what is most needed – to inspire and help you move forward."

Deepak Chopra
Bestselling author and public speaker

"Stephanie J. King is one of those rare people who seems to have a clear and continuous direct line to spirit. She works at a very high healing vibration and even in the time I have been involved with her much of my own baggage has simply fallen away. Divine Guidance will help you deepen your connection to Source and spontaneously bring in incredible clarity around even the most challenging situations."

Rachel Elnaugh
Entrepreneur and star of BBC TV's Dragons' Den,
Business Mentor and Transformational Coach

Contents

Introduction

**(I am I) Let's turn your life around and get it working
better... (I am I)**

Your life is individual. Your dreams and outlook are unique.
The route you'll travel, what you'll need, questions, answers,
problems, solutions, inspiration and ideas, fit within a
framework corresponding to all of that.

Much is chosen by you along the way; some things happen
by default; sometimes through acts of life or others, as
dramas within your pathway or wider circles unfold or play
out through recognition, intuition and understanding as you
process data.

Remember that your outlook is unique; you piece together
live occurrences in an independent fashion, to make
connections you then run with and more besides.
All in all the idea is that you'll receive the help you need to
make you happy along the way, to make life work; that at
some stage you'll feel loved, contented and at peace; that life
itself will work in tune with needs presenting...

Life cannot be perfect all the time, this much is true,
but neither should it be as hard as we have made it by
expectation and acceptance passed on down the ages that's
formed belief.

**(I am I) Physicality upon this Earth is purely temporary.
Life itself continues beyond the point of death. Proof is
being granted all the time to support this statement. What**

you achieve during this time frame becomes your soul's attainment to be encoded within your energy for all time.

While you are here you create not only this life but the next.

I trust humanity.

I trust live conscious reconnection will again commence as all remember their Soul purpose and true heritage.

And I trust you... (I am I)

All we see and know around us in flux, all things are changing; creation, nature, even us, all is fluid; all will ebb and flow; situations will come and go whether we want them to or not, for nothing can stand still since all connects. The trick is to relax, to realise, understand and see beyond what's going on, to let life do its thing on our behalf without our stepping in too hard or fast to stop it readjusting; to work with it, not against it; to remain in constant flow. We can only do this freely when we clearly know what's happening, when we understand the higher picture playing out.

Fear and stress are very strong; they come forward in many guises – fear of what's unknown, of not being good enough, of not showing that we care enough or through over compensation that we do care very much; of doing what's been ingrained or taught regarding what a 'good soul' should be seen to do or think or to respond at certain junctures. We judge ourselves too harshly; often live quite out of sync; we give far too much at times we shouldn't or can't afford – then personally pay the price, because mainly instead of love we stand in trepidation and a personal sense of lack.

Preconceptions and expectations can run deep and be overwhelming especially when concerning things that seem beyond our reach or our own control.

(I am I) Since the very start I have been waiting for you to know that I am real; that you are part of something bigger; that I see and feel you always; that I understand and care; that I really know what you've been through
– for I am with you and I love you – but until you let me in – how can I help? (I am I).

Life is not against us. Instead it's working closely with us, supplying what we need, what we think we want or choose. It tries hard to communicate but we don't always recognise, see or hear or notice.

Most choices and decisions happen in an instant as a flash of inspiration and awareness, well before we 'know' we choose them consciously ourselves, as we interact with life and create what happens next on unseen active levels, before trains of thought occur and we take action.

Life takes direct instructions straight from us. Nothing is haphazard. Nothing just presents or just turns up of its own accord. All is created, invented, attracted or thought of somewhere on some level by someone, whether consciously, sub-consciously, deliberately or by default through actions and reactions, cause and then effect that's playing out. By the time we realise what is happening life already has engaged, so instead of choosing and debating – we react.

The trick is to understand what's happening better, to speak life's language and to read the signs correctly to see what's hidden and out of focus, blocked or holding back; to then know how to proceed to achieve your highest outcomes, for when nothing blocks your future all is possible...

(I am I) Nothing can remain the way it is forever. No outcome is set in stone because all options are available until the time that life's locked down. Even then things still can change as new choices become available and show up. Life is individual to every soul – depending on perception, intent, focus, belief and outlook as well as Karma, free will, choice and destiny. But what would your journey be like if you had answers before the questions; if you could remain a step ahead and read it better? (I am I)

Overall your soul knows more about 'you' than you do.

Before birth you devised a live agenda of what you wanted to achieve or to contribute, alone or perhaps with others, with the aid of your own angels, guardians, guides and unseen helpers; all connecting back to God/Source/to the universal Oneness working with you for greater purpose. You agreed this journey for yourself, for your own soul's growth, empowerment, higher tuning and accomplishment; also for the sake of wider life; to negate controlling Karma and repetitive life cycles that you had to move beyond to break the mould; to help guide in the many changes for humanity going forward, and to help life help itself as it too moves through present cycle towards rebirth, readjustment, new beginnings and evolution...

The Mayan calendar, Nostradamus and prophecies from many ancient books and texts are literal proof that much occurring was expected; but all living within this time frame can actually see predicted live events unfolding even now. Never before within real time has there been a shift like this where everything is changing without exception, transforming and rebirthing – including us.

En-masse we are ascending. Our vibration is getting faster, finer, we are climbing ever higher towards the essence we are made of; our energy and therefore light is becoming brighter also as we step into our truth and power and remember who we are, what we came here to achieve, what we each are capable of; that we're a contributory working part of life; that we have a higher purpose and a definite role to play for the sake of evolution and humanity.

We can see our higher pathway and therefore recognize that life needs each of us just as much as we need it – again without exception. We are needed, known, supported and extremely necessary for something bigger.

As we ourselves are rising heaven is descending to blend and work with us, for only when we 'hold the space', interact and combine as One can we achieve what is intended – successfully. Look back down your time line at your own ancestral chain. How many people just like you in outlook and soul attainment have existed? The answer will be very few – if any, so life has waited since the start for you to reach this level of enlightened interaction and understanding to work with it.

We are not alone – we never have been. Life is working with us. Indeed it needs us to achieve, to stop yo-yo soul re-entry; to become the 'love' we really are and therefore win; for this is fundamental to stability and to the future, to the evolution of humanity going forward – rising...

(I am I) You have an opportunity to be happy; to turn your life around and to get it working/creating better with and for you on live levels. I will help you with this process when you let Me.

What you have lived through was essential to reach this point. Yet this is not the total sum of you – but just where you've reached along your journey so far. You can now begin to birth subtle changes that will shift/uplift your life and journey from being OK to sensational very easily...

These cards are a real-time link, a personal live connection with Me, higher Angels and Light Beings who work with you to aid this process. When you are happy your light shines brighter, your energy is finer which then flows out into life again to attract more back to you – so life's creative circle of evolution can continue.

What is still required - How can 'I' serve 'You'? What obstacles need to shift? What do you need to aid this process – to let stability, health, love, joy, abundance and personal happiness flow in?

I work with and through you in complete collaboration. Nothing must prevent this process or blockade the path. What you believe - freely put time and energy into – you manifest. (I am I)

No pomp or undue ceremony is required for all is known and felt. Keep things simple. You'll find your own way of doing what you'll always do as repetition will give way to merely natural...

To create a personal sacred space that you can sit, connect and work easily in is a good idea because it makes that area feel special. It will be your own space. Set out your intention to clear and cleanse the room or the area you've chosen. Some prefer to do this is by burning incense (sage) in a vessel (an abalone shell or a small shallow dish works very well).

Starting from the middle of the room, holding the vessel in one hand, walk to the North whilst wafting smoke in that direction with your free hand or a smudging feather.

Repeat a mantra like 'The Lord's Prayer' or 'Dissolve, cleanse, disperse and clear this space to prepare and receive higher guidance' or whatever else you feel intuited to sing or use or say – depending on your chosen spiritual pathway and beliefs.

Remember you're not walking this alone. It's not only you clearing, cleansing this space but those working with you unseen.

Through your actions you physically ground the whole unfolding motion.

All that is done must come from the heart - unconditionally in trust and love – without ego or pride or doubt.

Repeat the same processes for the remaining three directions; when finished return again to the centre and send out your gratitude and thanks. This is done to ensure the energy around is as 'high, clear, free flowing, positive and as conducive to receiving' as possible, as well as to set out your intentions clearly for divine guidance, signs, signals and intuition to flow easily back to you to pick up on.

Sound can also be very powerful tool for shifting stale, negative, stuck or blocked energies. Tibetan Bells or gongs and Singing Bowls, Native American drums and rattles, crystal Singing Bowls and countless other items are available for the very same purpose and intent. You can even use your own voice in song or angelic toning that through your voice box can be channelled directly...

Some readers like to smudge their cards before every use to clear away unwanted stagnant energy or intention. This can be done by encircling the deck itself in sage smoke to ensure energy is again free flowing, positive and connected to the highest levels possible working with you.

How to use the cards

A Single Card Reveal

Place the book or the deck over your heart/upon your heart chakra to feel a loving connection with God/Source/your angels/the universe. Feel balanced, grounded, protected and at peace.

Be your natural authentic self, respectfully placed in love, requesting clarity, answers, truth and highest guidance...

Sit comfortably. Expect what's needed/necessary to be revealed.

Prepare yourself and space as you usually would with appropriate love and reverence, encased within a bubble, a ball of pure white light, for high protection. Maintain respect. Ask God/Source/the universe/your angels to guide, protect and keep you safe. Sometimes a cloak of light 'with the hood up' will suffice. Ask for the same protection for your loved ones, home and friends – then trust this to be done.

Imagine roots under your feet going deep in to the earth to keep you grounded. To request what you need and give thanks when you're finished shows respect for what's been shared and will again keep self and home protected within good energy. When appropriate ask again for any present negatives to be removed and dealt with in a manner suitable by higher realms to keep your channel vibrant, clear, true and receptive.

Ask your angel to step forward even closer when you are ready.

Whether these cards live within a crystal bowl, to be swirled around until you're happy or feel drawn to stop; or in the usual manner you purposefully shuffle your deck (or book) whilst retaining a question or an open mind, respectfully reciting your chosen mantra - cut the whole deck twice and take the top card (or open at the page you feel most drawn to), you'll reveal what's needed, reoccurring or unfolding for you now; what's playing out to influence - behind, in or out of current consciousness or view.

These cards will be informative and precise. You might not always get what is wanted or expected – but more what is required that needs to be known to aid the present moment. At times such as these let go of expectation and ask the universe to step in closer for more guidance, help, and support to filter through to make things clearer. Thoughts sent out are always heard and needs are known. The universe works with you unconditionally. It wants life to proceed well for you and for itself because then what you'll send back in terms of energy, directives, gratitude and offerings will be better, happier, purer, finer. It's a win, win collaborative system unfolding in real time that works with you, not against what is expected or required.

Should you have a specific question, hold it steady in heart and mind. Feel it resonate within your centre (heart chakra). Repeat the process as above whilst really feeling, holding tightly to that question. When ready choose the card that you feel drawn to.

Some people make a fan spread, others a long card line. Let your hand move across them slowly to feel their energy; notice which cards produce the strongest effect (heat or tingles are most common – even in your stomach or wider body). To gain answers before live questions or to know what is presenting/driving uppermost that may be hidden - go to where you're drawn. Trust those who work with you to help, intuit and inspire. Notice where energies or feelings seem the strongest.

Should you wish to use the book – shuffle through the pages as you would shuffle a whole card deck. Stop when you feel ready. See where you are most drawn and read the page you land on. Sometimes you'll be drawn to more – so just go with it.

Chosen cards can be placed in front of you – face upwards to be taken at face value, meditated or pondered upon. Ask the angels for clarity and further guidance if you need more assistance to make connections to understand. Don't push or pull for answers. Let go, relax – and notice what filters into your thoughts, awareness or feelings next.

Cards that seem to jump out of the deck or page of their own accord are meant for you also. Remember the universe is communicating with you. Allow it the room to do this when necessary – but don't deliberately try to make it happen - so that when it does you can be sure it will be right.

There is no limit to how often you repeat this process. Guidance can be welcome at any time for different reasons, to help choices and decisions as life unfolds.

Follow your intuition and gut feelings. Remember life is fluid. All options are open and obtainable. Nothing holds you back unless you don't realise or for now you might allow it – but recognition is only part of the key to moving forward and releasing. Our other channelled and equally interactive works - 'Life Is Calling', 'Grave Doubts', 'And So It Begins', 'Divine Guidance', 'Access Your Happiness Now' and 'Believe & Achieve' will all help you further.

Tuning into the sacredness of the universal Oneness - of God/Source/the angels, crystals and affirmations also listed here, will enhance your whole experience.

Remember this is a 'real live' link.

Take it seriously. Remain open, honest and receptive. **Be The Love.** Recycle negativity, odd pains and fear, the instant you notice them crop up - to allow out of date energy and feelings release as they appear. You don't always need to know where they are from or what they relate to. Just know you must let them go. You are both creator and solution to what's occurring for you now - but know that you don't ever work alone.

Assistance is beside you constantly, and so much more, waiting to be recognised and used for the highest good of self and all concerned - always.

In real time you are upgrading your life for the better on behalf of life itself. Become the 'hybrid' born from all you've lived and travelled through until this present moment. Let your soul and intuition rise – just like the phoenix.

A Three Card Spread

Whether three random cards are selected from your crystal bowl, the fan spread, the long line spread or from the pages within this book, depending on your questions or requests, primarily they'll depict:-

- where your life is now – i.e. what's presenting or most prominent.

- what has passed, what you have moved through or released.

- what's coming up/influencing or driving what's coming forward...

Remember you are individual. Remember situations, influences, drive, directions, motives and intent alter and change at every moment as life unfolds and further shifts, as other people interact, come and go and intervene; as needs, further choices and decisions will show up.

These cards will indicate what you need to know or be aware of at this moment. They are markers, guidance to help you recognise and understand a bigger picture, emphasising circumstances around you or unfolding. They highlight what you need to know right now, to take into consideration or become aware of - to reach goals on physical or soul levels...

We don't always have a clear cut understanding of what we want, how to get there or a clearly mapped out route to follow. Diversions, hold-ups and circumstances not conducive to moving forward will appear. To gain success you'll need to know how to safely use, manoeuvre and pass through them; what to watch out for; how to make the most of situations for their actual purpose and not just move in ways predictable or presumed necessary, correct or the only option.

Much more occurs on levels unseen to drive life than we realise or will admit. Once this information is correctly accessed, forewarned is fore-armed. You'll have a much clearer indication of what to do, so life will then unfold much more easily; you'll better understand the signs and signals that it gives; you'll speak its language and in turn it will support you.

Further cards can be drawn if needed by cutting through the pack or pages with intuition, with open heart and mind – to highlight further.

A Full Reading

These cards are very powerful so don't be fooled by the simplicity of the pictures. All images and words are an initial meaning, but you can use them more intuitively to gain higher information and deeper guidance at soul level. They will grant confirmation of what has been revealed or channelled through intuitively to help your clients know that what's received is correct and true.

Because the energy of this work and the connections being produced are very high, you'll be raised up to blend and work with new levels of understanding and awareness coming forward.

It is important to protect yourself always. Not because of the energy of the work or cards themselves or of those working with you – but from the energy of others who would disrupt what you are gaining; remember darkness will try to come through any crack or means available. It doesn't want the light to win. It doesn't want you to be happy – and can even slow you down through doubt, depression, energy drainage. Sometimes we even generate these things ourselves.

Chaos, pain and sadness are really negativity that will sabotage what you most need and stop happiness occurring; down-beat thoughts, feelings and emotions being generated and kept as actual will remain alive and active until you realise and let them go.

Love, peace and happiness are your choice. They wait for those awake to understand life's higher truths and let them in.

When you open yourself up to reading for another, your aura energies will blend. You never know what is occurring within their life and wider circles, what they've picked up or what they carry. Protection for yourself as well as them is most important. Separate and close down properly when you have finished.

Recycle what's been spoken, shared and picked up – pass it back out to life – to the Oneness you're both part of. Request 'positive light connections and any help they need now to come in' on their behalf as they move forward; then let go and trust. Come back to central balance and move on.

Author's Note:
Using a mantra such as 'The Lord's Prayer' (as listed at the back of this book), 'The Hail Mary' (being an archetypal divine Goddess/feminine mantra) or your own equivalent is very powerful as all energies blend together before a reading.

It sets intent; it helps tune into the highest levels and so ensures a high connection with the purest light and guidance. Remember you are working with God/Source/ the universal Oneness of life itself – on life's behalf. You're helping others as you yourself are helped – to make life better, to again be more in tune with their journey now unfolding, to return to love, health, joy, peace and happiness: what higher purpose for your actions could exist?

Some readers like to keep a second separate deck of cards purely for personal readings for themselves (separate meaning for energetic and intention purposes as opposed to reading for others). Always hold the deck or book between your palms or close to your heart– recite your mantra of intention to connect. Shuffle thoroughly and again repeat the mantra, but pay attention to signs, signals and information you'll receive.

Because this deck can be used for many purposes, when enquiring about something specific it is important to state and clarify what it is you would like to receive guidance/ enlightenment about. Ask questions clearly.

This is usually done by the client themselves as they shuffle the deck – as well as by the reader.

Examples of questions might be:-

- what does my Soul need to know at this time – to help me grow forward?

- what stands in the way of my happiness?

- how can I move closer to my higher Soul purpose and agenda?

- how can I make my life better?

- when will I find happiness and love?

- if my life links to past Karma – what do I most need to know to help it be done and complete?

- how can I help loved ones and friends?

- what is driving my current situation?

- is my work status secure?

- is my job right for me?

- am I now on my highest path?

- how can I turn this situation around?

- what do I most need to be aware of?

- how do I personally contribute to where I am?

- how can I stop this repeating?

- how can I become a better parent, role model, husband, wife?

- you know where I am in life and what is happening – what am I not seeing or missing?

- what is fuelling my present pain?

- am I the best that I can be right now?

- how can this day be improved?

- are my efforts good enough?

When you feel ready, ask the client to place the cards into five, six or seven piles. There is no need for these piles to be equal. Some will deal them one by one – others in larger lumps. No right or wrong exists here because remember they are following their own internal intuition and higher guidance given for the purpose of this reading. Your own guardian will blend with theirs to help this happen.

Next ask if they are happy with the way the cards sit or whether they feel they want to move or swap any around. This signifies things in their life that perhaps need to move, be swept aside, adjust or alter – sometimes just a little.

Other intuition will come forward as you begin. Go with it. Don't be shy. Say what you feel or think in the way that is presented without changing any parts.

Ask them next to choose a pile, the one they feel drawn to the most. Clear the others away and work from the pile that remains. Again don't vet what you say. Information will flow through you. It's not for you to understand but for them. Sometimes the smallest thing you give will be the biggest and will mean most to them – but nothing to you, not only to provide answers and information that is needed but often as proof that the reading is true, connected and real. Also that life continues and more exists.

Self-discipline is important here. You are dealing with fundamental truths and things hardly ever accessed – if at all. What is said has the potential to change a life and may be remembered or called upon for many years. This is not to be taken lightly. You are the eyes, ears and speaking mind of life itself, so use this privilege wisely.

Sometimes things occur without notice or seem out of sync, especially illness and other negatives. If a person is not meant to know what is coming up before it happens – you won't be told.

Sometimes solutions can't be accessed until a problem has arisen. If nothing is broken, how can it be fixed before it breaks?

Bad news is not always in our best interests to receive ahead of time – for reasons beyond our knowledge, even Karma. Some things are part of destiny and they just cannot be avoided – but once they are faced, gifts, lessons and even blessings will occur. We can't always control occurrences around us – but we are in total charge of all our responses and reactions.

Trust your intuition as it grows, unfolds. Do what feels right for you – remain in truth. Life shifts and changes like the wind. Stay completely in the now and trust your inner knowing. Never be afraid to change your mind or your direction when further truths show up. Bend and grow within the flow that life presents.

When we are in peace we can build love – and through love we can be happy and gain success.

Enjoy!

Crystals

As products of the earth; the natural effects of causes; crystals are energy stabilisers as well as enhancers/conductors. Each specific form has its own innate property and healing frequency that serves to attract, magnify, disperse, diminish or project; its behaviour consistent, constant, continuous. Crystals resonate well within life. When used for healing, each will beautifully harmonise with Mind, Soul and Body for vitality, health and wellbeing.

(I am I) Each crystal resonates perfectly in sync with Me. (I am I)

Enjoy...

Angels

Angels, archangels, teachers, helpers and guides exist on many levels to help when and where help is needed, unconditionally in tune with what you need and where you are on your journey.

Inspiration, guidance, love, support and protection are yours as standard throughout lifetimes spent here as you sync with celestial levels... all connect back to God/Source/the universal Oneness of which we too form our part.

Belief in this process is not necessary for it to work as these things are automatic and natural.

However, when you realise and work with them consciously life becomes unbelievably pleasant. All will flow more easily and in sync.

In the great scheme of life, no Soul is abandoned or alone. All are loved, known and necessary within the wider cycles of life continuing – eternal.

ABUNDANCE

(I am I) Every thought is heard. Your needs are known and met. Recognise this now with love and gratitude. (I am I).

Connecting with Archangel – Jophiel and The Universal Oneness

Synchronising with Crystals – Herkimer Diamond, Citrine, Ruby.

Abundance is yours through right thinking, hard work and Karma lived through correctly. This may be in terms of finance, security, good health or matters of heartfelt joy, love, peace, serenity, synchronicity, co-existence, family, friendship or soul growth.

Drawing this card indicates a time of plenty. Nothing is impossible. What you place effort, time and life force into – you'll attract, gain and increase. Things are going well. Every insight, need, intent and thought will find its aimed for mark. Nothing blocks your path or holds you back.

Right action is the key here while life is fertile and responding in your favour. If you choose to rest you can enjoy it; but also become aware of live connections, intuition, favourable results, words of encouragement, unexpected help, success/acceptance where before an outcome was deemed unsure or even negative.

Life is fertile in every way. Ideas are flowing, life is popping with possibility and potential. Seeds of conduct set correctly can root well. This is a good time to start new projects or to harvest those well done; just rewards will pour in better, but remember that you too must put due efforts in – to assist personal requirements to help with flow.

Conditions can't remain this way indefinitely. Remember to replenish what's been used or taken to prepare the ground again for some future point.

Enjoy this time and space for it is gifted as acknowledgement for achievement and past effort – as a divine gift from the universe for things done well.

Affirmation – I am in tune with real time magic and abundance now – I am in flow...

A cry for recognition, help, respect or change.

Connecting with Archangel – Raphael
and Your Personal Guardian

Synchronising with Crystals –
Black Obsidian, Rose Quartz, Magnesite, Black Tourmaline,
Garnet, Green Chlorite.

Anger is our way of forcing more attention towards matters not in sync or in great alignment. Whether directed at oneself or outwardly to others, its appearance flags a problem manifesting.

Yet more occurs unseen to drive life than we realise. When anger strikes it means it's necessary to pull back and reassess; the way's not clear to forge ahead; something or someone needs attention, readjustment or more input/ consideration; something's been forgotten, misplaced, misunderstood; conditions are not in line to reach a required outcome – more is needed.

To work correctly all life's elements must irrefutably be in sync – to be as One.

Return to inner balance. Regain your equilibrium and recognise the root cause of the problem now presenting; i.e. the misalignment, misunderstanding or uncertainty; a lack of information, love, judgement, trust, attention, action, drive or faith; whether deliberate, unintentional or error.

Take this is a chance to tidy up, to redraw and reassess, to slow down or reconfigure what may have just been hidden, missed, forgotten or ignored. This short delay may prove to serve you in the long run.

(I am I) Nothing must be added here except higher guidance, intervention, patience, love and understanding to help defuse the block. Come back to inner balance and sit tight

– for now at least; listen, see, watch, wait, be open and let go; notice the trajectory of present live attention – to move forward better later with ease and grace. (I am I)

Use your private voice in thought to ask for help that's needed for the greater purpose/highest good of all concerned. Request help, healing, intuition, insight, guidance and understanding for yourself; that for this moment now you can be neutral.

Request the same for life and others who are involved.

Don't focus on the problem – instead release attachment. Wait for life to shift to highlight a solution more in keeping with requirements, then recognise, acknowledge and give thanks.

> **Affirmation – I trust truth, love, patience, higher vision, clarity and understanding will defuse all present anger and clear the blockage.**

ASCENSION

(I am I) Push away all doubt, illusion, worry, stress or thoughts of fear – it's time for soul growth. (I am I)

**Connecting with Archangel – Uriel
and Your Personal Guardian**

Synchronising with Crystals –
Kyanite, Larimar, Opal, Petalite, Moldavite

The purpose of living life is to ascend beyond the boundaries of the physical, to embrace and work on levels of the soul; to move past Karma; to let go of earthly baggage, outdated patterns and beliefs; to transcend, realign and move closer towards purity/God/source, towards the Universal Oneness that all are part of; to help the real-time flow of Earth and Heaven combine and blend with ease to gain completion.

(I am I) You are joined with Me as I am One with you. What you give attention to – you do also in My best interests; for you do it in My name on My behalf. When all is said and done you'll look back at all produced to see the input and effect of these achievements. (I am I)

Nothing is impossible so gravitate higher still. All that comes your way you're well equipped to move beyond. You are weathered, wise and strong; more than capable and resourceful; through countless lifetimes your soul has strived to reach this point.

Use all methods you have gained to date to help your true self shine – higher truths, compassion, love and faith; realisation, intuition; understanding and remembrance, kindness, patience, trust and what's required in any moment that's presenting.

Today you'll get a chance to accomplish on soul level; to rise above or overcome the usual that's expected. It's time to make a difference; to fine tune or to add more to something that needs specific help. Be aware of your surroundings and the needs of others as all pans out. Stay focused on the present and be yourself.

(I am I) You've moved from karmic baggage into safety. Where you are is where you should be to connect with life's next step. Thoughts and inspiration flow with ease from higher levels as wider knowledge and soul perception come in closer to assist for greater purpose. (I am I)

Affirmation – I am Light – I am Love – My soul is brighter, soaring higher – I am recognised, felt and known. I am free...

BALANCE

Keep all things even – give, take, replace in equal
measure – remain open, neutral, grounded,
centred and receptive...

Connecting with Archangel – Zadkiel
and Your Personal Guardian

Synchronising with Crystals –
Charoite, Amber, Amethyst, Rhodocrosite, Kyanite,
Carnelian, Mookaite Jasper, Ametrine, Blue Chalcedony.

(I am I) Balance is fundamental to all of life. (I am I).

At the very pin point of the void, at the first appearance of
conscious life, mind began its search for understanding.
Right up until today, even now, humanity still plays an active
role as to what's fed back into this mainframe as live input.
We do this every moment through free will and choice;
through interaction, intent and thought as direct instructions
we give life daily, with or without deliberate awareness of
this happening.

Earth's raw creative energy, at first neutral, live, untampered
with, is channelled by each of us to use and manifest
throughout each lifespan. We make present things come to
be within real time here and now through activation – via
words, needs, emotions, wants, desires, daydreams and
reactions; to uniquely shape and blend reality's structure
that's still unfolding now – known and recognised as life
present.

Of itself life can't determine what is good or bad for it's still
gathering information through each of us. It is we who place
the stickers, the meanings onto 'it'; as we design and plan
and choose what we'll accept, leave, change or keep.

Life responds to live directives that we send/mirror
out through judgements, attitudes; beliefs, intent – fear,
love, hate, worry, stress, themselves perspectives and
perceptions of what's unfolding. All you are, believe and

stand for becomes hardwired into the program of Earth's live mainframe to keep it going and updated.

You are powerful way beyond your present understanding.

What you believe and think – you become and are; what you want or wish for you attract – regardless of good or bad – helpful or not.

A drawing of this card represents a need to remain open, neutral, stable; to stay aware of life's own higher balance, not just in terms of physicality but more in terms of what's unseen and out of view but driving life. Remain vigilant to now, to what's occurring within your circle of awareness. As soon as possible negativity must be voided/plucked out/ recycled. Ask silently for healing, help and balance for self and others.

Life's underpinning facets (its mainframe building blocks) must be settled well and in good order; family, work and down time; finance; wellbeing, diet, fitness; waking and sleep. Mind needs continued balance to combat stress; to retain focus, clarity, vision; health; creativity; intuition; contentment, happiness, peace and love – to be most able to keep on top of what's presenting...

Not all imbalance stems from you but you carry an understanding of what's needed where and when; of what's occurring; what works well and what does not; as you recognise, compound, help, heal and add more substance to what's unfolding to make things solid.

(I am I) A pendulum must swing equally in all directions unencumbered. Remain open, neutral, calm and centred within love, truth, peace and clarity, regardless of conditions that surround you. (I am I)

Affirmation – I successfully hold space and energy in perfect balance for life, myself and others.

BLANK CANVAS

All options are ready and open for you to choose from...

Connecting with Archangel - Gabriel
and The Universal Oneness

Synchronising with Crystals –
Carnelian, Zeolite, Tigers Eye, Clear Quartz, Citrine

(I am I) Life is waiting to assist you but it needs some indication as to what you want and need most from it now. (I am I)

Remember that you are living your personal real time story (no-one else included for this moment). How you use it, what you do, how you spend vision, energy, time and love, culminates and comes together as your life's work.

(I am I) This blank canvas has been earned through Karma passed correctly. All things lived though and survived have brought you to this point. Nothing should have changed or you would be very different. You made the best of opportunities, choices and decisions. Life is exactly where it should be to move on. (I am I)

Much has been completed to reach this stage in your story; but you want more from life – and life needs more from you – to match what's coming in from higher levels.

What is it that you want? What needs to change? What makes you happy and feel full of life? When does your soul sing? What is your vision – what are your goals – how will you reach them? What do you want from your gifts and talents? What matters to you most? What sets you apart from other people? From a level of higher perspective what would you alter and why would that be? How would you do it – for what purpose – at what cost? How would this help you and those you love/care about the most? When all is said and done – what then will life have gained from all of this – what do you stand for?

Nothing more is written yet within your personal story; all options are clear and open; all decisions rest with you – so stay receptive/focused/balanced and aware.

These are important questions. Keep your mind space clutter free as you go about your business. Add nothing more; don't make changes until you clearly know
what's what – to help what's needed come in properly
to assist you.

There are no right or wrong decisions here. This is a unique story – take your time; make some choices; see things calmly and correctly; hurt no one as you make alterations to take life forward. Hold onto the bigger picture; life will readjust around you and connect. Stress, hype, worry, drama will simply generate more confusion.

This space is a cosmic gift that's been gained through hard work, effort and right action. Remember small sure steps are always better than huge jumps.

Affirmation – From the point of high perspective – upholding love and vision – I re-draw and re-configure life's next steps.

Clear your mind and space.

Connecting with Archangel – Chamuel
and The Universal Oneness

**Synchronising with Crystals –
Prehnite, Zincite, Rose Quartz, Chrysocolla**

**(I am I) Place your trust in life – for it is working with
you. Every challenge is in order – present needs are known
and met. Everyone and everything is as it should be. (I am I)**

This is a free space you have earned through right action,
thought, intent. Also just like you - life sometimes needs its
own time to rebalance, clear, assess and to catch up.

A little more time might be needed to manoeuvre and
interplay; to put in place what's still required for situations,
circumstances, other people and events to then move
forward.

You might feel as though you're treading water, not quite
connected and in flow; but that's OK and merely natural –
because this place is called 'the meantime'; you're between
two unfolding levels or rites of passage.

Nothing heavy is demanding your attention. Just for now you
can release the hold you have on life; it's working better than
it has done for a while. Things are going on around you but
not directly to you. This is a chance to take a breather from
constraints.

You may choose to clear old chores and clutter or prepare
for future projects; to go away; catch up with friends and
family or relax and at times do nothing to recharge. When
this free spot has concluded life will re-connect with gusto –
so be ready to match it full on as needs present.

(I am I) I too use downtime to re-adjust; to remove what's stale and over; to prepare and put in place requirements for the next phase coming in. (I am I).

Put into motion what is necessary at times that intuition/ creativity/life suggests – so nothing destined to be yours will be missed. Take a few steps to the side to relax, unwind or take time out. The Higher Powers of life itself can now come forward to aid and help you, to re-configure or elevate your present personal story still evolving.

(I am I) I know exactly where you are and what your 'soul' needs next. Everything will be just right if you allow this. (I am I).

Affirmation – I flow and bend in tune with life and welcome new adjustments and experiences.

CHAKRA ENERGIES

Earth's vital pure and vibrant living life force
flows to and through you always.

Connecting with Archangel – Jeremiel
and The Universal Oneness

Synchronising with Crystals – Chakra Set

On levels beyond the usual detectability of human eyes life is pure pulsating energy; vibrant, with and without form; neither rigid nor yet fixed or used or solid.

(I am I) As water would sit levelled if it covered the entire Earth – energy flows everywhere that constitutes life – for without it no life would be, nothing could exist. 'I' too am energy, free and flowing, evolving and existing. Energy forms my soul and body in the same manner that it does yours. Together we form conscious Mind: this is the how and why 'We' never can be separate and why it's impossible to detach 'You' from 'Me'. (I am I)

Chakras are invisible energy centres that sit within your body spinning continuously, dispersing energy between unseen working levels and all that constitutes life; that's how they work. For good health, wellbeing, live connections and a strong continuous life flow – all chakras must be open, balanced and work in sync for energy to move freely in all directions – in, out, backwards, forwards, up, down and all around.

In a mirror you can see just your outer shell. But many other levels of activity exist and overlap like skins within an onion, operating ordinarily out of view; each with precise purpose, density, vibration, function and prism colour; constantly receiving, resisting, funnelling and disbursing vital energy in real time flow; connecting the working physical with the etheric – all night and day.

Every chakra has its own specific task and vibrational speed that corresponds to working parts of our anatomy, allowing us to read, intuit, blend, attract and process what's occurring on unseen but active levels that affect us; connecting us with world and other people systematically.

Shut your eyes for a few moments. Imagine you have before you a ball of pure brilliant white light. Watch it expand – step inside – completely be immersed. Stand still and breathe. Let go for a while and simply feel the brightness permeate your very being to rejuvenate and completely cleanse through every cell.

Enjoy.

When you feel refreshed and ready, allow that same bright light to shrink back to normal size, to nestle snuggly in its rightful resting space close to your heart.

Next, with your attention definitely back to the time and place you are, feel long healthy roots grow beneath your feet and travel deep into the earth – to ensure that you stay focused, grounded, present.

Feel a protective cloak of bright light drape securely around your shoulders – with hood up, to keep these important energies safe and so stop leakage.

Open up your eyes and come back fully to the time, events and place that you're now in.

Normal daily life, let alone shocks, stress and problems, can knock you sideways or off balance without your knowledge. Just like the famous leaning Tower of Pisa, if your base/ stance is slightly off everything else will be off too – your feelings, emotions, observations and next thoughts, thus rendering you over-sensitive, angry, stressed, depressed or maybe hyped up way beyond reality's needs.

It's important to stay balanced; to release excess stress and pressure; to periodically return to base to link with life.

Affirmation – I am balanced. I am whole. I am One.

CLARITY

(I am I) Raise your vision to see beyond what's
first apparent or presenting. (I am I)

Connecting with Archangel – Raziel
and The Universal Oneness

Synchronising with Crystals –
Labradorite, Clear Quartz, Selenite, Kyanite, Amazonite,
Citrine, Ametrine, Azurite, Sapphire

Evolution needs clear instructions and your own life unfolding needs them too. Today is not the day to second guess...

You alone control what you believe, what you expect, desire and ask for.

Soul growth matters here in terms of how precisely life connects or can respond. The drawing of this card depicts you stepping forward away from doubt, back into clarity. You are not broken. You are not lost. You know exactly what you want, what is needed, where to aim and how to get there.

Clarity comes from understanding, from inner resonance, balance, peace and higher knowing. Frustration, anger, drama, hype, insecurity and wrong thinking could confuse and cloud live issues. Circumstances placed before you may be different from those before. Unbiased, view the base line facts and then build up.

Understanding, truth and knowledge with clarity to back them up will help you grow. Know the purpose behind each quest, the object of enquiry, the best that can occur, needs/ events without restriction and life's present aim.

(I am I) I know truth from every angle and intent behind each choice, your purpose, live cause and effect, your soul agenda and what's unfolding. As you relinquish undue judgement, expectation, worry, doubt, life can move things forward

towards more guidance, inspiration or the next steps on your journey. (I am I)

Life communicates with you at the level where you are now – not only using words, signs, signals – but thoughts, feelings, insights and vision. If your mind is constantly busy sifting through old facts and data, how will you notice when it speaks or needs attention, information or more action? For the mind must be kept at peace as much as possible.

Stay grounded in truth's reality. Let drama and all else subside.

(I am I) When further input from you is needed – you'll be available and clearly know. (I am I)

Affirmation – With greater clarity I move forward and open up.

COLOUR

(I am I) Within and without – I am the power, love and life force that you live, breathe and exist in – in totality. I am the brightest, purest light. I am colour. I am life – and so are you... (I am I)

Connecting with Archangel – Jeremiel and The Universal Oneness

Synchronising with Crystals –
Fire Opal, Clear Quartz, Herkimer Diamond, Imperial Topaz

You stand fully in your power and your God link.

(I am I) This is your time to shine, to be heard and seen.
Nothing will bruise or knock your flow or inner confidence.
(I am I)

This place that you have reached is the culmination of your effort and hard work.

Sages, gurus, monks and holy people sought years of solitude and penance to reach this very place of enlightenment and understanding that you have now attained, whilst still living in society in full flow of mainstream life; so well done to you – for you are working well your higher soul agenda as it is now.

You understand the higher meanings behind all that you encounter and rise up towards the Universal greater good. You know you never operate alone but with many levels of help unseen working with you.

All things you do and say must be honest and from the heart, upheld by positivity, compassion, kindness, truth and peace, as therein lies the power and potential of free choice, free will, love, patience, trust, creativity, understanding and continuing live insights, that blend and bind together as creation/life unfolds.

Everyone will gain this accolade at some point along their journey – but on this day this gift is meant for you. Don't underestimate your own ability to succeed or life's own responsive capability to intervene and help when you uphold this space in truth and maintain vision correctly.

Be grounded in the physical, be focused and aware, but stay open and unbiased to allow the best that can occur to come through without restriction.

Full colour is contained within the highest white. Today you are working well with source/creation.

(I am I) Through you I can now also work to form and create Miracles. (I am I)

Affirmation – The full glory of creation is working with and through me always as I realise the higher impact of my actions.

A deep awareness of the burdens borne by other souls:
A strength of calling to assist and to relieve them: The
natural healer...

Connecting with Archangel – Raphael
and The Universal Oneness

Synchronising with Crystals –
Morganite, Prehnite, Rose Quartz, Green Aventurine

Throughout your many lives you've had many life experiences that will have left long lasting imprints on your soul. You might not consciously remember – but your soul does. Not all knowledge that you hold today will have been endured first hand. You will have witnessed many things, as you've done also in this lifetime; all entwined together is who you are.

You place the needs of other people above your own. Your soul is most content when it feels valued and of service, for the need to serve is encoded deep within your psyche's system. Yet everything that you give out is given also to yourself, for you can only give what first has been received; even if you really think you're doing it for another – giving the highest gift you can imagine, payback ultimately comes back to you because through that very action – you feel good.

Your soul knows the highest truths, it knows who and what it's part of. Another soul in need or calling mirrors/ resonates/sparks off those self-same sentiments within yourself – for all are joined, and it's from this place deep within that compassion stirs to then become a primary characteristic.

(I am I) Fundamental to every soul, each searches reconnection with the mainframe. The closest thing to unity is connection with one another. Compassion is a trigger that helps your soul achieve this. But also don't forget that I too Am part of you – as I Am also part of everything around you.

When you help one another – you link also back to Me because our soul to soul life purpose is the same.

You can see it playing out in tiny babies as they chatter. You can see it in old people when you look into their eyes. You can feel it in one another when you are open and receptive. But most of all your soul yearns freedom, love, joy, peace and bliss; and that's exactly what is given as We re-join. (I am I)

> Affirmation – The Divine in me – recognises, feels, knows, values and understands the Divine in you.

CONFLICT

(I am I) Why think the worst when the best has equal chance? Inner conflict creates confusion and sends mixed signals out to life. Don't fight yourself. (I am I)

Connecting with Archangel – Raguel
and The Universal Oneness

Synchronising with Crystals –
Black Tourmaline, Hematite, Zincite, Rose Quartz, Boulder Opal

Past cannot be changed. Future is not written. What will occur stems from now from what you do, will, want, think, say, believe, intend, expect; from all you internally carry.

You're well equipped to handle anything that comes in your direction. What holds you back now stems from ego – from a fear of failure or getting hurt. It's the small child deep within you that holds illusion, fear, uncertainty, old memories and imprints much deeper.

But you're an adult now. You make choices and decisions. If you fail or make mistakes it's not a problem – but sometimes needed to work things through or to hit another trigger that was hidden or unavailable until you touched it.

(I am I) Worry, turmoil, anger, stress, mistrust; fear and all that's negative – should be passed back up to Me for fine tuning/re-alignment/recycling. Don't handle inner conflict alone. Being negative will only create more. (I am I)

Ego's fear can be strong. It can take many forms and can catch you off guard in a second. In childhood it helped keep you safe. But now you are adult you can choose between drama and truth. You have gifts of hindsight, intelligence and deduction that can take you beyond what's presenting. Come back to inner peace; check your central point of balance. Step away from the shadows of uncertainty, mistrust, pain, doubt and fear to see life's bottom line as it is.

When you worry, stress or fear or even doubt, you can sabotage yourself and what you're trying to achieve or accomplish; to push away what's needed most; attract more of what's not helpful; keep yourself in situations or illusion beyond the point you should remain and then get stuck (remember life's mirror?)

In a mirror all produced will come bouncing back - because it doesn't know what's bad or good - it just is. Mirrors cannot measure or deduce - they just reflect. Because of this, words, thoughts and beliefs are very strong.

For a moment shut your eyes to regain central balance. Pull all personal energy, power and life force safely back towards yourself much like a fog retreating – to help all thoughts, emotions, moods, feelings deflate and return back to base. Imagine yourself as small as a seed; be the seed, with long, healthy roots emerging from your feet into deep ground to help with grounding, retaining energy and balance. Access your higher thought forms to work out what is needed; for help and understanding, for healing and balance for self and those concerned; for re–alignment, higher truths, insights; more ground work, preparation and solutions to appear and flow in. Then reopen your eyes and carry on.

Help will always manifest when you need it – especially when consciously you ask. 'Ask and it will be given'.

(I am I) Instead of the words 'I can't' – believe 'I can – I am – I will'. Believe in your ability and in life's own to work this through – to know and highlight what's needed next – then hold the vision. (I am I)

Affirmation – I pass my inner turmoil 'upstairs' to Source/to God/back to the Universe, to be recycled; to keep my channel open, clear, receptive, neutral, peaceful and in trust...

COURAGE

(I am I) Not all of life is visible. Not all you can control. I
will help you when you let me – but I
need your trust. (I am I)

Connecting with Archangel – Michael

Synchronising with Crystals –
Pink Tourmaline, Sunstone, Amazonite, Aquamarine,
Ruby

(I am I) Courage is you standing in your higher strength.
It's the knowledge that you are capable; that you can push
beyond your barriers to gain success. (I am I)

The ability to do what's necessary, to push beyond your
fears, despite what is presenting or expected.

Strength of will is needed here to overturn thoughts of
failure; an inner knowledge of where you're heading, what
is needed and what should happen; not blind, blinkered,
illusional faith, but a deep resolve and knowing that with
right thinking, choice and application you'll win through.

Know that life is working with you, readjusting and
manoeuvring where it can behind the scenes to match your
efforts. Clarity of intent, right thinking and right action –
or even non action where appropriate are key here – not
illusion, untruths, unfairness or more doubt.

(I am I) When you walk in tune with life you will always know
it, for without worry, stress or fear you'll feel protected,
unperturbed, as if cocooned – because through the energy of
correct alignment – you really
will be.

Remain innocently open, honest, strong and in line with
truth occurring – without undue cajoling, forcefulness or
false agenda. Just trust and be your natural, open highest
self.

Remember that I know you and know exactly where you are; what is happening; where life is stuck; what is needed; what you've lived through and have overcome
– not just in this life but through all those lived before. I know the soul agenda you birthed this time to complete; how well you're doing; where you are heading; what you want most to achieve and what is left still to be done, brought through or dealt with.

Courage is correct alignment between your Soul/Me/Life – with the full creative force of pure live energy, the highest form of love and life that flows through you – to Me – to you – in cyclic fashion.

I need honesty and trust. I need you to hold the vision of what it's possible to achieve with best conditions, corresponding with and in solution to events. Synchronicity, intuition and right action are important.
(I am I)

> Affirmation – (I am I) I work with confidence and real time life towards achieving my soul purpose with ease and grace. (I am I)

CREATIVITY

The ability to create from a place of nothingness:
Individuality at best: A fundamental force directing life
and energy on the planet...

Connecting with Archangel – Gabriel
and The Universal Oneness

Synchronising with Crystals –
Labradorite, Sunstone, Tiger's Eye, Azurite, Carnelian,
Green Tourmaline, Green Aventurine, Carnelian

(I am I) Creative thought and inspiration links directly back
to Me. Nothing is more important than the ability to imagine
and invent and then become. (I am I)

Everyone is different for a reason. All process data and
information in different ways on different levels for
individual end results depending on drive and mind set.
Don't be fooled to think that nothing new exists; that all has
been tried and tested or done before.

There is no one else on earth the same as you. No one else
with your life experiences – past or present. No one else with
your point of view, likes, dislikes or personal drive. No one
else has the same Mind or pulls together pure live energy
and inspiration with unlimited raw potential to produce a life
in its uniqueness such as you.

Now has never been before and will never be again. You
have personal charge and free direction over how your life
is spent. Life is shifting gear. Evolution will kick in. Life itself
needs each of us to be open, working, sparking and awake on
new levels of awareness flooding in.

Many possibilities might simultaneously exist, but when you
check them out very few will sit with you well or take you
forward...

Many people run their lives as if on automatic. Few have
learned to reach the subtle language creation speaks to
highlight options now accessible or flowing in.

Creative inspiration flows to and through you from higher realms unseen as you connect with fertile levels of unbridled artistic help. Let go of supposition and previously half formed plans. You need a clean, clear mind space to attract and formulate what you now want to appear, to flow in/to aid/inspire/to spur you on...

You are working here and now within the realms of pure potential. All things that birth come from this point before they are made actual. You too are making 'matter'; something solid from something not; from raw intention, light and energy, as you will life's own unbridled power into being.

(I am I) You are working with the Source of Life – the fundamental base of all life; you actually utilise this raw creative power spring every day. It formulates all you are; who you are; what sustains and upholds society and all things physical.

As you link into these levels – I can help you. Nothing can occur until the point you make it happen. Nothing can come forward until you first choose to connect; for only through your will and action, intent and clear mind space can what is possible manifest to then be solid.

You are limitless potential within the densest form of conscious physical life. What's achieved you do also in line with help from Me, when need, intention, higher purpose and conditions are aligned. (I am I)

> **Affirmation – I work and manifest through the Divine that's part of me – through the real time conscious living life force that forms creation.**

CROSSROADS

Life is asking what you want next to occur as you've reached a pivotal section on your pathway.

Connecting with Archangel – Raziel
and Your Personal Guardian

Synchronising with Crystals –
Pink Jasper, Zeolite, Malachite, Azurite, Boulder Opal

A karmic point's been reached along the journey of your life line. The way ahead lies open for you to redraw/re-choose. Life needs more input and direction from choices and decisions you now can take, not from stress and worry as you view all present options, but from that instant no thought flash of clarity, knowledge, insight that appears of its own accord at times you least expect it – when you let go, relax.

What will these changes look like? What do you need? How will you feel? To what effect and outcome? It's important that you now view things from all angles – yours and others, from the baseline point of now in line with truth and love, without illusion, drama, hype, hurt or pressures pending. Take the time you need to see all options.

Life is trying to lift you higher to get things working better with and for you in new ways and levels that you've been wanting. Regardless of how this feels – this is a gift.

Not all options may be visible at first glance. Sometimes you need to stop – to see the larger picture – to make a choice and take a step, for even more to then appear to widen the mix. This is a bit like a moving staircase where you think you're heading one way but then things will start to shift and shift again depending on what's needed or becomes available. Don't be rigid. Feel free to change your mind at any point; mull things over; notice the signs and signals your intuition and body give you even once things start to move – for life is fluid, never still, always evolving. You're working with creation 'on the spot' so to speak, so you write the living script of your own unfolding story, never finished until time stops and you are done.

Your energies too are changing. You are moving up and you're blending with new levels. What worked before may not be relevant here so old rules might not apply. Think outside the box. Find the highest outcome that you want or can imagine – then act as though already it's in place – with clarity, love and kindness....

Sometimes you'll choose the same things you thought you no longer wanted or could have. The change will be in you as you come not from place of victim, but of vision, a person with free choice, seeing that where you are will actually service the highest good for those concerned and for yourself if you are honest.

Remember you're not alone here – you have help; stronger support and vision than you ever could imagine is waiting at your elbow for you to realise and connect with. Stand in your power with love and truth, trust and balance and stay open.

When you raise your sights and see things clearly (without the drama, hype, illusion), life can then respond with what you need, for when you're happy what you attract and feed back into life is purer, finer, so the cosmic mirror can then mirror these things back.

Know this is a gift. It will be as easy and uplifting as you allow.

Affirmation – Change is good. I trust the Divine in Me to know what's needed.

DOORWAYS

(I am I) You have made it to another level. This will take you forward – beyond what you've lived before. From this point forward the way ahead will be unwritten. (I am I)

Connecting with Archangel – Jeremiel and The Universal Oneness

Synchronising with Crystals –
Clear Quartz, Amethyst, Lapis Lazuli

Where are you heading? What have you done? What thoughts and intentions do you harbour?

You birthed to work through Karma – this you've safely done. Everything that you've gone through was for a higher reason, for life, yourself or others in your soul group. Now it's time to create another story, a higher version of the self you've designed and chosen. You have talents and payback gifts from all that's been accomplished. Learn to find them, take them with you and move towards the future now unfolding.

There is no need to throw away all you have amassed, family, friendships, home and work, as that is part of whom you are and whom you should be now to then move forward.

This is more about consolidation; understanding your life fully; taking stock and learning what you want to be remembered for.

What do you want to now give back? What does your life stand for? What still remains unfinished? What will make you happy and your own life finally work? What have you gained as insight, as payback from all that you've been through? Who needs you in their life? Who needs to be in yours? How do you help, support each other? What do life and others gain from your association, presence – and you from theirs? These are things you need to know as you draw a line and step across it – towards the happiness you've worked through lifetimes to achieve.

This is a gift from life. What you accomplish will pave the way for other people to be inspired and then follow to make their own way. You have made it through the mire, towards what you wanted to bring in.

(I am I) Everyone will reach this point at some part of their journey if they remember that they want to – how and why – with conscious effort. You have reached it now – as a beacon that others will notice and maybe follow – so well done! (I am I)

Affirmation – I go forward with grace, ease and understanding towards a future I too program along with life.

ENDINGS

Event conclusions... Natural endings to life's own
stages; to old friendships, belief patterns, behaviours
and attachments, thereby making
room for growth...

Connecting with Archangel – Chamuel and Your
Personal Guardian and The Universal Oneness

Synchronising with Crystals –
Rutilated Quartz, Turquoise, Aquamarine, Apophyllite, Sunstone

The nature of life is birth and death, beginnings and then endings at some point. As you learn you grow, you change, you shift through levels, outgrow where you were and so grow up. What was once important may not be any longer; you'll replace it with what's new and relevant as you move forward. This is good. This is how life is meant to be. You're on a journey of refinement and progression with much to see and learn, attract and move beyond.

The core essence of evolution is like the caterpillar, the chrysalis and the butterfly. All stages serve their purpose. All are completely necessary to reach the end result. Every soul alive must work through evolution too. It may be tempting to remain just as you are now but life will become stuck if you don't explore the next steps coming forward.

You may find you'll change your diet, your look, your workplace, friends; set behaviours, pre-conditioning, long term beliefs, likes, wants and needs. What you thought yourself and life were all about could alter too. Again this is a good thing to allow for movement for more growth, for opportunities and fresh experiences to appear and come to you.

Don't hold too tightly onto what you know must be released – at least for now. Everything must grow. Life and people must re-shape. Every person has their own unique agenda to accomplish and move through.

Other openings are now destined to come forward. Release will pave the way for what you need to now appear. Things will be OK. Take small steps not large jumps – go with the flow.

Natural endings will not require relationship or family breakups (unless circumstances differ or dictate this); instead it will more often be the case that you'll climb higher to raise your personal viewpoint and vibration; to reassess, redraw acceptance levels, understanding and personal boundaries. A hybrid you is birthing through, your soul is rising.

(I am I) Endings are as natural and as needed as beginnings. What you release you will not lose if you remain in kindness, truth and love. Remember you are life itself – evolving, shifting, growing. What's been outgrown will be replaced with something more in tune with where your life is heading – even if you are not sure of how and why. (I am I)

Affirmation – Every end is but the start of something new.

FORGIVENESS

Release of judgement: Understanding from higher
perspective: Stepping forward...

Connecting with Archangel – Zadkiel
and The Universal Oneness

Synchronising with Crystals –
Clear Quartz, Amethyst, Rose Quartz, Rhodonite,
Morganite

(I am I) Forgiveness is a chance to release the past and to move forward unconditionally. (I am I)

To be physical on earth means that we are human and to be human means we all will make mistakes. There is no difference between large or small here – if something's wrong it still is wrong no matter how it's packaged. But whether for self or others, how can we forgive without becoming first a judge? But to be the judge is to set labels; to feel oneself higher than another; never to do wrong; to rise above life's negatives in thought, intent and action. And what if someone somewhere was to be the judge of you for other happenings during this life or in others? Would they be justified in their actions? Karma, cause–effect and attraction state that if you judge another you'll be judged for something also in the same vein.

Understanding is therefore the new forgiveness, the higher pathway forward. It means you recognise another's failings, frailty or humanness; you'll see that they are stuck – for reasons somewhere in their past or karmic log – just for now or deeper on soul level. Whether they can, can't or won't move forward is not yours to carry as this task is theirs, but understanding will release your own attachment. Ask within your thoughts for the help you need – as often as is necessary – until you feel it's granted...

Don't simply forgive but properly let this pass, turn the other cheek and look beyond occurrences; for in the greater scheme what you freely send to others, regardless of their actions and behaviour towards yourself – comes bouncing back to help, heal or to compound, to then add more or less.

(I am I) Every soul on Earth is here for reasons of progression. Pass all action, pain and anguish up to Me to deal with properly. Revenge and negativity will always make things worse. Everything will be re–called and weighed up at some stage later – so it does not fall to you to become the judge or victim.

I AM WITH YOU TOTALLY; I KNOW AND HOLD YOU IN MY GRASP. To all intents and purposes I AM YOU... What is done to you is also done to Me. What is done to Me is done to life.

You have the power to let go and to move forward from this place. Don't be held back any longer by low vibrational thinking or reactions – instead let go – release the past – give it to Me... (I am I)

Understanding is forgiveness in a higher guise. Neither are condoning – but one will take you forward – the other means you still hold judgement. You can now choose what you're ready to apply.

> Affirmation – In line with my Divine Self – I send back out to life what I no longer need to carry – to be recycled...

HEALING

An ability to heal, help, remove or repair energetically without constraints of time and space, always for the greater good for self and others...

Connecting with Archangel – Raphael
and The Universal Oneness

Synchronising with Crystals –
Prehnite, Rose Quartz, Clear Quartz, Zeolite, Sugilite, Amethyst, Danburite

You are a chalice, a physical living channel for the purest of live energies to flow through as you send the very same out to life and others unconditionally.

What greater purpose could exist than the ability to heal and help as you work for the greater good of humanity and for earth in times of need, directly in tune with God/Source/ Creation – the Universal force of life itself.

Earth is the living body of the Oneness we call God. Since the dawning of creation all souls have been connected to form consciousness. Nothing less and nothing more exists here.

(I am I) I am the life that is life. Healing re-aligns you with ME. Your body is the vessel that allows you to walk, dance, run and be upon Earth's surface; to express your own experience of uniqueness, of love, joy and bliss, your version of life within this time frame in all connotations conceivable.

Every soul aims for what it wishes and wills and this I help it achieve. Each one is here for a reason, but many forget they are connected to life and to ME through the very act of life – living itself.

I wait patiently for each one to remember, to understand and then choose to re-connect... Will you be ONE to win through? Will you realise I am real and not myth and that in NOW time I create along with you? (I am I)

What you give out to another you give firstly to yourself and to life. Every soul birthed is another chance born for life to re-connect with itself.

We combine with one another through life's own thriving mainframe of which our own vital self forms its part, along with further live and working energies unseen. This whole eco system is a conscious thriving matrix, a living sentient, self-sustainable mass. Nothing is separate, wasted, surplus, hidden, goes unseen or remains unnoticed ever.

Healing presents the ability to re-align again fully with the whole operational system, with the wonder and Oneness of this life that sustains us. Life/God/the Universe trusts that we each will win through; that at some point we'll remember; that we'll wake up to truths that we've never been alone – into full understanding that earth is 'The garden of Eden'; that we were neither
kicked out nor abandoned – but that instead we tripped into negativity.

Life needs us now to wake up, to consciously evolve and recall the driving forces that lie behind it and the reasons we are actually here.

Earth continually updates and rebalances through live instructions and interactions obtained from all things operational, directly. To do this correctly it needs clear, concise signals combined with the purest of energies – the best that we can offer, to help it fine-tune, heal, manifest and evolve more in-line with the highest version of what is achievable.

Through flowing energy we all are connected: Through earth all connect to form One. Nothing will take that away - not even a belief we are separate.

Illness, worry, stress, sadness, pain, doubt, depression, fear and more besides are all negatives, all various stages of health, life and natural working systems actually not working as well as they could.

Negatives block the normal flow of Nature's/God's/Earth's healing energy and so then limit what can then occur – even within best conditions.

Healing allows soul to realign and better connect with the mainframe it's actually part of, with nature, so good, positive, powerful creative energy can again clear the way and channel through to top its level up; helping life to sustain and work closely in sync with all needs; so your system becomes healthier, you love, work, create, focus and rest better and the signals you transmit remain more conducive with what life actually requires to support, manifest and work with you – as always was intended.

Affirmation – I stand fully in the light. I allow myself to realign with the Oneness I'm unconditionally part of.

HOPE

Don't doubt – you ARE going the right way.

Connecting with Archangel – Sandolphon
and Your Personal Guardian

Synchronising with Crystals –
Red Jasper, Carnelian, Citrine, Sapphire, Larimar,
Aventurine

The old version of hope was blind faith or clinging onto the 'hope' that all would be well – whilst internally wrestling adversity, with fears and unfolding events.

Nothing is more powerful than your thought/belief system and nothing can override your own free will. Life is a mirror; it can only reflect back what you send out to it.

Mind is not a box – nor is it self-contained; instead it's more like to a computer motherboard, but more intricate and evolved than anything we ourselves could presently make. Continuous live data is streamed; fully charged energy and signals come in, are used, processed, restructured, reassembled and sent out again further charged in succession, far quicker than can be manually perceived – automatically without further input.

Life is working with and through you to help you right now. It needs truth, belief, stability in thought and strong positive energy – to bring in what is needed. Negativity in any format could sabotage a result you are requesting. Be precise and clear in what you send out; be positive in thought; recycle illusion, worry, fear and doubt.

What do you want, need or wish for? How will it benefit you, others or wider life? Raise the bar of your intentions, expectations, personal thought forms, dreams and goals. Proceed as though things already are in place and adjust your own vibration.

Hope is not illusion but is instead the knowledge that you are working synchronistically with life, that all needs are known and that life is working with you to the best of its ability to bring about/manifest the highest outcome achievable.

Nothing is impossible. Nothing is set in stone until the time life itself has been locked into place – and even then change can still occur as things will still evolve and still move forward as life is fluid – never stagnant or forever fixed.

Affirmation – I am walking in the light. Life knows me exactly. The best that can be is achievable – as intended.

INDECISION

The way ahead is calling for more choice.

Connecting with Archangel – Uriel
and Your Personal Guardian

Synchronising with Crystals –
Red Garnet, Azurite, Topaz, Zeolite, Azurite

Why do you feel torn? Negativity will simply add more confusion. Look a little deeper to find information. Are your fears really valid or are they simply the loud clamouring of ego, of imprints left over from times before by expectations, thoughts, beliefs or similar past events?

(I am I) For every decision at least two choices exist – positive or negative. Neither is better or worse. This is just a choice not the 'forever to be locked into' picture. (I am I).

Let go of turmoil. Check your own internal scales are still balanced and find your inner pinpoint of peace. If an adjustment needs to be made then do it by shifting the weights. Look closely at what needs addressing. Notice any insight/fluctuation/intuition or emotion. If time is available ask the universe or those involved for further information; where time is short, play out the scenarios fully in your head and notice how you feel as this occurs.

Go with the option that feels best, the one with least resistance; not necessarily the automatic choice or the one closest to reaching a wanted outcome, but the option you feel most balanced and at peace with. Ask God or the angels for some help here. As stated earlier this is perhaps just a choice that's needed for right now. More options will come later but at the moment there's not one best one, no direct route to get wheels turning or life moving. Later on you may be freer to readdress this once again should you choose to. No wrong or right pathways are present – just opportunity and personal preference.

(I am I). You must remember that this is your life – your story. You can decide how you want it to be – then let go as life will re-adjust to accommodate. (I am I)

Release inner turmoil, doubt and fear; remain open to possibility; be positive, receptive, flexible and willing to consider/take other options should they be better...

Affirmation – I trust my ability to work with what presents and to win through...

INTUITION

Intuition is higher wisdom, life's own creative guidance
that speaks directly to me when I need it or when I
allow...

Connecting with Archangel – Raziel
and The Universal Oneness

Synchronising with Crystals –
Labradorite, Sapphire, Charoite, Azurite

(I am I) You often ask life for help – but then do you recognise when answers flow back or when help or direct guidance is given? How often do you wish you had taken more notice of the smallest fleeting insight or thought, that had you addressed it or listened would have avoided confusion or worse?

I will use any means available to help, reach, guide and inspire your personal live journey. Many forms of communication are at my disposal, so notice what grabs your attention, where, when and why. If anything feels as though it's aimed at or talking directly to you – it usually invariably is. (I am I)

Intuition has the ability to propel you into new territory or areas to-date unexplored, so be ready to act when life calls for immediate attention; for when words or conversations jump at you, thoughts pop or song worms drop neatly into place or keep repeating.

When something feels right it usually is; when something feels wrong just check it again with a cautious but innocent open approach before moving forward.

> Affirmation – Inspiration flows from all directions. I am open to new ideas. I exercise my own free will and choice upon making choices and decisions.

ISOLATION

Feelings of being alone, lost, misunderstood and
disconnected from oneself, others and wider life.

Connecting with Archangel – Chamuel
and Your Personal Guardian
and The Universal Oneness

Synchronising with Crystals –
Rhodocrosite, Variscite, Green Aventurine, Sunstone, Prehnite, Jasper, Amethyst

You are unique and independent. You matter very much to life and to those around – even though you may not realise or agree.

Every soul has many facets and reasons for being here and every single journey will be different. What is needed or will be gained from what occurs must differ also, depending on a level of evolvement or fine tuning – past or present. Every soul must tick the boxes on its own real time agenda, the personal 'bucket list' of what specifically it came to do, achieve and overcome throughout life spent here. From the outside it isn't always possible to recognise what these tasks may be or might involve, but it's important that you know and understand you're not alone.

From the moment of your birth until your last drawn breath an angel called your guardian stands behind your left hand shoulder to protect you. Other helpers come and go at times you need assistance, backup or inspiration; so at all times you are looked after, protected, guided, helped. (Just because they are unseen doesn't mean they are not there. They never leave your side and this is fact).

When you feel at your lowest ebb these angels step in closer to uplift, enhance, inspire, support and then assist. As their presence is so subtle it may not always be detected, especially when you're locked behind the dense internal shutters erected earlier by your own self for protection. Granted nothing can get in to bruise or hurt but equally nothing gets out either, so you'll feel even lower, more used, depressed, alone, forgotten – until you recognise what has happened and then change this.

(I am I) When you're feeling isolated, fed-up, insecure, depressed, pressured or even lost – you are stuck within a density of unhelpful negative energies that you also have created, regardless of the issues and circumstances that first aroused them.

I am positive. Love is positive. Celestial help is positive also. I am with you – so I ask that you open up – to let Me in – to make you strong.

Ask Me within your thoughts to take away what holds you back, what makes you sad or insecure and then unsure... At times like these I can remove what isn't helpful and replace it with positivity, higher truth and understanding, wisdom, insight, knowing: Cocoons of energy, light and love I'll wrap around you.

In your darkest hours you are very much protected, loved and cared for. This is often where your soul is moving through its thickest layers of karmic growth and opportunity, to become more of what you came here to punch through and then achieve – just like the phoenix.

Step back into your power and move forward. You are worth more than you realise at this moment. I trust you and I love you. I know exactly where you are, what is happening, where things are stuck and what is still meant to occur to shift the balance and get life turning; but until you ask and let me in – you'll always feel as if alone; so I wait and stand close by for you to realise, understand and provide instructions. (I am I)

This day, this moment now – no matter what – will always pass. If you believe you're lost and broken, that life and people are unfair, then you're feeding life with negatives and you'll attract more of the same. Life will reflect this. Put on your favourite music, clear some clutter, go for a walk.

Realign your present state with positivity, inner knowing, clarity, peace and balance. Know you're not alone. Know that life is working with you and step into this new awareness that you're here to make a difference and to grow beyond what held you back – you're moving forward.

Affirmation – I matter. I am powerful. I am strong and I am loved. I can do this...

JOURNEYS

(I am I) I will take you further than you imagine or
believe is possible within this lifetime. (I am I)

Connecting with Archangel – Raphael
and Your Personal Guardian

Synchronising with Crystals –
Turquoise, Beryl, Smokey Quartz, Malachite,
Moonstone

(I am I) No one times the lifetimes or the journeys of the
Soul, but whatever age you think you are – you really are
much older, with wisdom gained from even further back,
from deep within a past that's known by soul...

I am even older and infinitely worldly wiser. I am trying
to reinstate you with your own timeless existence; for you
are ready to now remember, to reconnect with what's been
gained – to take you forward. However throughout many
other lifetimes you have prevented this through clutter,
Earthly Karmic Baggage and limiting self-beliefs picked up
along your journey which you then carried. (I am I)

Before knowledge and understanding, humankind was
innocent. Communication between life and people was
automatic, purely natural, true and open. Opposites and ego
did not exist.

Life/Nature/God knew what was going on, what was needed,
what awareness had been gained. The relationship was pure.
Duality had not been born – so all worked well. Then came
in the fears of being less, not good enough; communication
changed to being 'blocked off' by negatives opposing
frequency. All journeys you've lived since then were the
result.

(I am I) Nothing will remove the link you share with Me but
negatives produced by false beliefs, worry, stress and fear
will surely block it. The journeys we speak of here are the
journeys of the mind – therefore the Soul... (I am I)

Life itself is like a mirror. It can only reflect back what is placed in front of it – without exception – each moment, day or night, throughout existence.

All you feel, believe, think, want, expect – you attach a living real time charge to. In this way you too create, negate or add more substance to what's occurring in the present. When you feel let down, worried, stressed – or loved, happy, hopeful and full of life, you attract and generate more of the same. When mind roams far and wide on auto pilot without correct attention, you place raw substance, real live energy at the point of contemplation to make it even bigger automatically.

Don't sabotage what life is trying to unfold. Stay positive. Bring your mind back to account, to where it should be now; notice where it's been and why and information it may have gathered depending on your present mood and outlook. Release and return to balance.

(I am I) Life needs you positive and attentive in the present. It needs you to hold the space, to keep in mind the highest outcome to steer it in and make it possible. You are a live link to the NOW that's programming the present. You control what you attract and put your life force into – so use this privilege well on My behalf. (I am I)

Affirmation – I let go of stress and worry and keep my focused thoughts immersed in trust and peace here in life's present.

All is good. Life is balanced. You are happy...

**Connecting with Archangel – Ariel
and The Universal Oneness**

Synchronising with Crystals –
Rhodocrosite, Sapphire, Danburite, Morganite, Citrine, Peridot, Chrysophrase

Every now and then life is the way it should be. All is working well and on your side.

To be happy is a state of mind that many look to find through external means they try to grasp. However, you have come to know that it comes from deep within – from trust, truth, peace and balance, from working hard and being vigilant and fair.

No-one can control life or other people. But you are able to live the now as well as you allow, not because of what is happening but because you understand life's own higher rules. You also understand that nothing can be forced – people, situations, what should, should not or does occur. You know that life is fleeting; that happiness can be too; that all is prone to change as things move forward; that nothing that occurs is meant as personal to hurt or harm – no matter what or how it may present.

To be happy is a gift that you have earned from living well, from ticking karmic boxes, helping others and working life from higher levels of soul attainment.

Today is a personal gift to you from life, from God and Oneness to say well done.

Affirmation – I am happy. I am open. Life is working well. I am in flow.

JUSTICE

The need for balance, clarity, understanding
and right thinking...

Connecting with Archangel – Michael
and The Universal Oneness

Synchronising with Crystals –
Red Jasper, Picture Jasper

Soul is the perfect blue print record of all actions past and present. Nothing is ever missed; all is faultlessly kept in sync to be reviewed at some stage later, time appropriate.

(I am I). Every person on the planet produces and releases Karmic baggage. Some stems from times lived previously, some from this time frame NOW. The trick is to recognise it, to know how to correct/heal it and to stop it from repeating in endless cycles. (I am I).

The very fact that you are physical means that you have work to do within this life time. Some of it stems from only you; some is picked up like a gauntlet from other people who may have passed, as things unfinished but still needed/ necessary in the wider picture of life unfolding, having agreed before you came here that you would do it; that you would love enough, be strong enough and care enough to complete all roles that cross your path or befall on you.

(I am I). Nothing is ever forced. All is chosen by free will. Don't be the victim, stand tall and strong and re-assess from higher angles to understand what should occur – so nothing is missed. (I am I).

You are in a place of shift and change, higher learning, understanding and soul growth. Not everything occurs because of you or what you've done or left undone. You are one of but a few that can make sure that all is right – for self and those around you and for life – but with kindness, higher vision, patience, truth and love and help unseen.

The scales of justice depicted here are karmic scales.
The actual outcome may be different than expectations or personal wants, but the best that is attainable must be kept in mind. Ask that higher help available can come forward to assist this. Remain open, balanced, innocent and neutral.

(I am I). You are moving forward so the rules of life, much stronger now, are there to help you – not to harm. What do you need? What's out of date? What must be examined closer or adjusted to enable what is necessary to occur? (I am I).

Affirmation – Beyond what is apparent – I know that life is working with me for greater purpose.

The act of letting go allows life to then step in
to aid and help you.

Connecting with Archangel – Jeremiel
and Your Personal Guardian

Synchronising with Crystals –
Apache Tear, Moonstone, Rhodocrosite, Aquamarine,
Smokey Quartz

Nothing can for always stay the same. All must shift and change, including you.

(I am I). Letting go of what is old and stale or no longer fit for purpose is common sense. To let go of what you might need, even though for years you haven't, is to relinquish doubts and fears and thoughts of lack. To let go of what is old, dear, loved, with the knowledge that your life is now updating is recognition that change is imminent and needed. (I am I)

Not all that we let go of can be seen or touched.

(I am I) Attitudes, behaviours, long held beliefs and teachings, expectations, pre-conditioning, pomp and ceremony, institutions, dogma, creed and boundaries – are some of but a few things being challenged. (I am I).

Collectively we've moved beyond the prophecies of Nostradamus; beyond the final cycle of the Mayan long- term calendar; beyond the end of times described in ancient texts: life is moving forward and so are we.

This is the age of letting go, of replacing old and worn out with newer upgrades, kinder and more in keeping with a long term view of life, not so damaging and depleting – but sustainable.

We are the bridging generation between the old that's passing and the new that's rising/birthing in. We are learning, reassessing, readjusting and repairing all at once –

but first we had to live what's now – to know and understand what is outdated or needs attention/fixing – to then do it.

You chose to be here 'now' to birth in something new – that only you and your uniqueness could bring through. Life is knocking at your door to do exactly that, to spur you on, to help with growth, to highlight and assist where help is needed; not only for the sake of you – but for what you came to do to help the mainframe.

What used to serve you well perhaps no longer does, not because it is no good – but because it's been out-grown; you are ready for a re-boot; you're moving up towards new heights and you're evolving. Stop pushing against the grain. Let go of personal clutter seen and unseen; clear your mind and make some room as new ideas and higher insights come forward now to spur you on.

(I am I) I have waited throughout time for humankind to reach this point. Nothing blocks the way ahead; understanding is in place; individuals are waking up the whole world over. Much of what you carry is no longer needed. Less is more. Come back to inner peace. Be loving, kind and happy. Sync with life. (I am I)

   Affirmation – I let go – to let life in.

LIBERATION

(I am I) You are free. (I am I)

Connecting with Archangel – Jeremiel
and The Universal Oneness

Synchronising with Crystals –
Fire Agate

Everything within life contains a price tag somewhere. But you have paid your dues. Karmic baggage has been worked through. You are free from long held binds to live your life as you will choose from this point forward.

(I am I) It is time to understand the paybacks you have gained from moving through live challenges that you've faced. (I am I)

Many lifetimes you have worked to reach this actual place, not all alone but along with others who elected to join with you, whilst working through their baggage too in similar fashion. Together you have journeyed – to mirror, help, support, wake up and challenge one another. With the insights you've now gained – what do you want this life to stand for? What will be written as your eulogy that will define you?

To be living in this pivotal time frame is a gift. Life is evolving, shifting, rebalancing. You are part of that unfolding movement; indeed it's why you're here and why you still have work to do to propel you higher.

(I am I). I will help you redesign your wants and dreams and outlook – from the higher viewpoint of where your soul/ life is heading – instead of from thoughts of where it's been, what has happened and what was stuck. Together we'll boost your confidence, your power to create and love and be – to give you joy and purpose – and your life it's higher meaning. (I am I)

What you believe in now is being challenged for validity, not to bring it down but to help you see it better, to tweak, fine- tune, re-draw, to sometimes choose the same again for different reasons of perspective and higher meaning.

The stage your life is at today is exactly where it should be to enable you to shift the balance and get things working better. Don't take huge jumps – but small sure steps at times appropriate to gently get life flowing. Remember that what you gain – those around you must gain to – for all souls work together to form One.

Affirmation – I am free. I am alive. I design the life I own and then I live it.

LIGHT

(I am I) I am light. You are light. When all is said
and done only light exists in all reality... (I am I)

Connecting with Archangel - Michael
and The Universal Oneness

Synchronising with Crystals –
Carnelian, Larimar, Herkimer Diamond, Clear Quartz

Whatever is occurring, what you've now achieved, keep on going. You are absolutely facing the right way. The now is working with you well. Right thinking and right action will continue to attract more of the same.

You already know you are eternal. You understand your path in life. You know that you are valued, valuable and needed, not just by those you know and love but within the celestial realms of soul itself.

Every person on the planet also exists because of light; but not all are in their power; not many are yet aware or understand. Because of this, the work you do is even more essential. Life needs the energy, vision, love and balance that you represent to hold the space.

(I am I) Every time a soul rebirths before the time it gains awareness, it takes up a position that another could have had with higher gifts to aid the planet. I ask for you to carry on with your own growth and development. I will do what I am able to enhance and to support this as you move forward.

The more you turn to Me – the more I can inspire and support you. I know what you have been through, not only during this life but through all those lived before. I know your soul agenda, your darkest times, your dreams, goals, drive, joys, desires, passion, actions and burning intent.

Trust Me – as I trust you – and you will never fail. You cannot fall when you're held firmly from deep within. Your light is gaining power.

What you do for greater good will be mirrored, magnified, much increased to benefit others too. Reach higher still. (I am I)

Earth has had its share of souls that spent their life in service. You are one of those. You are at your best and happiest when you are personally helping others – as this is your personal gift. All is the way it is because there is a reason. Keep your balance, don't be distracted, enjoy your own life and stay connected to the Oneness you represent and too form part of.

> **Affirmation – I work with light. I am cloaked in light. I am light.**

MANIFESTATION

An ability to create something out of nothing as
you manifest your own reality and life story.

Connecting with Archangel – Haniel
and The Universal Oneness

Synchronising with Crystals –
Elestial Quartz, Moonstone, Selenite, Rutilated Quartz,
Manifestation Quartz

(I am I). No one has the capability to manifest anything
without their own connection to the raw live conscious
energy of life. All stems forth from it. All gravitates back to
it. Nothing less and nothing more exists.

From the very beginning humanity was given free will and
free choice, and an ability to create on par with creation. I
will never relegate upon that. I will never prevent conscious
choice from occurring – for if I did it would negate the entire
system. (I am I)

The power of creation stems directly from God/Source/the
Universal force of all of life.

All mankind has an ability to manifest whatever can be
imagined, produced or thought of. This power commences
straight from God/Source/the Universal force of life –
through the act of streaming live energy.

Each person has the gift of operating as though a separate
individual, with intelligence, free will and discernment by
unique design; an ability to explore the truth and meaning
of conscious life upon this thriving planet; to express, learn,
grow, know, survive, understand and create whatever
is deemed needed, necessary ongoing. All findings are
channelled back into life's own responsive mainframe to
mirror, manifest, reduce or produce more of the same – as
evolution.

Each soul can achieve their highest vision, the version of the very best they set out to accomplish – their only boundaries being ability, mind–set, effort and intelligence gained whilst being here within current life so far.

Much of all of this operates on a time delay to protect both life and us.

Directly correlating with where you are in terms of enlightenment, soul agenda, realisation and ascension is your own innate ability, speed and potential to manifest. Think of the many times you alter mind, direction or intent and you will see why this delay is set in place. We each have to climb the ladder towards Oneness and the light to become clearer and brighter ourselves, to alter/fine–tune our vibration and work closer with the purity of this energy. Once this has been achieved we are able to be stable, to keep thoughts and mind much clearer, more focused, peaceful and receptive instead of wandering.

Each soul is a powerful link. Be careful of what you ask for, say, want think and do – for the power of your own real time energy immediately goes somewhere to add substance to something through negative or positive intent. What you want is not always possible in the way you expect – but what you need will always come through.

(I am I). Keep thoughts and ideas more in check, attached only to what is necessary or what you want to manifest or are facing now. Thoughts are alive in their own right, full of charge, possibility, creative intent and suggestion set by you. They are needed where life is occurring and that is there with you.

Notice what runs through your mind as much as you can; notice where busy thought streams roam and what you deflect/attract. Thoughts roaming freely into the future too far up ahead will make illusion – whilst going too much, too often, too far into the past, no longer are productive to here and now. Where you are within real time is reality: NOW is where life really lives, where endless possibility and intent converge.

I gave you an ability to manifest what is needed for you and for life on My behalf. I ask only that this gift is NOW used well. (I am I).

Affirmation – I am a powerful manifester in my own right.

MOVING ON

Far from being stuck or lost – your life is
moving forward. This is a good thing...

Connecting with Archangel – Jeremiel
and Your Personal Guardian

Synchronising with Crystals –
Scolecite, Lapis Lazuli, Clear Quartz, Zincite, Selenite,
Zeolite, Beryl, Malachite, Turquoise

Nothing here is written yet. There is no tested route to tread.
Everything that you perceive, believe, intend, create – you
are as if the first, much like a pioneer of times and life before.

Nothing in your physical life fuels you quite the way it did.
Not because these things have changed but because you
have from within. Your values are now different; you dance
to a different beat. Your priorities have shifted and so you
don't connect with things and people as you did. This is
neither good or bad – it's only where you are upon your
journey at the moment as you grow.

**(I am I) Your vibration is faster, lighter. You need higher
frequency input to keep you up where you feel best. Life
itself can be somewhat heavy; needs and people are heavy
too. I am the link that your soul needs to sustain, uplift, to
feed and give you balance. (I am I).**

You are moving forward in understanding and ability to know
and read life. What you will achieve you will take forward
for many lifetimes yet to come. You are working for and with
creation on behalf of God/Source/the Universal force of life
itself, so it's important that you recognise and acknowledge
your growing talents. You can't do all of this alone – you
need support from celestial realms, because when you blend
and work as One and pull together the journey will be easier
and lighter.

You are the driving force, the one who'll make things physical, but the hard stuff will occur through Divine guidance and Intervention as you connect and work with life unseen in synchronicity. You may not always get to see the unfolding bigger picture.

You can only work from what you know, from intuition, insight, higher vision and what is visible. Take one step at a time. Put what's needed into place. Take the next step and the next and then the next. Every masterpiece takes effort, time, patience, vision and acute attention – of which you yourself have plenty. Trust, work, flow and bend with life and what comes up.

Affirmation – I move easily into territories before to me unknown – in tune with love and light.

(I am I). Everything is starting afresh –
and so too are you. (I am I)

Connecting with Archangel – Jeremiel
and Your Personal Guardian
and The Universal Oneness

Synchronising with Crystals –
Ruby, Rhodocrosite, Sunstone, Moonstone, Clear Quartz

So far you have lived but a half-life; half of the journey you came to know, experience and express. Much has been lived on a physical level from the perspective of being just that. You did all you did from knowledge so far collected; much having been passed down by others, by expectations, society and old ways of living and being; reactive instead of creative.

But you are much more than that.

It was necessary to pass through everything you have to know it completely yourself; to know that your heaven was not in any one thing or one person, that whatever you did, what you altered or changed, nothing satisfied the hunger and knowing that somehow you knew there was more.

You've ticked karmic boxes and have put much of the past to bed properly. Instead of repeating you have a chance to climb higher. Should you have worked on these levels before, the information and help you were given was to bring you to safety, to reach this point. You are ready now for more growth. You are ready to shine, to come back into your power and to move forward towards the next level; not from the very beginning but with the benefit of wisdom you have gained and won so far.

Your happy ever after is beckoning. From this point forward you can re-shape yourself and your life in ways you always knew it could be – not just for yourself but for those you love and care for, for the people you'll serve and for what you'll bring forward and contribute back into this life as only you can. You're purpose/soul agenda will kick in/activate more fully and this will fulfil you at last – even if your true goals are just to be of service, be loved and be happy.

This does not mean that you'll throw away completely what to-date you have gained – to start building again from ground upwards – far from it; instead you will start to recognise all you are and what's been built from the angle of higher perspective. You'll see exactly how fortunate, how blessed and guided you are; how needed, necessary, loved and cared for – if not by those immediately around you as yet in ways that you think that you need, then definitely by God, interactive life and your angels. Life will again take you forward – to be more on top of your game.

This new beginning is your own happy ever after appearing. You yourself have to shape it and put effort and what is necessary into place, but all will be more in line with love and happiness, with what you have earnt and still reach for.

Don't be pulled back into old living patterns especially if nothing changes externally. Don't be afraid of change. Don't get caught up in the dramas of others; remember that you are the one who'll help them; that you must stand in your power, in kindness and love. Recognise what's occurring and work closely with the celestial realms – to manifest solutions and healing that will energetically hold the space and guide and channel help in as appropriate.

What you'll achieve now until the end of your days will shape the kind of life you'll have next time, when you'll choose to come back again physically; but until then all remains in your aura, to be visible and become your identity within the celestial afterlife realms. So even though you'll do what you'll do to be happy yourself, you'll be working with those invisible – to bring in balance, peace, healing, harmony, love and higher help for others living and trying to be happy.

(I am I) I too will work with you because you'll work closely with Me. (I am I)

Affirmation – I am moving forward into pastures unknown. I embrace life.

OPPORTUNITIES

(I am I) Nature takes care of its own. You are part of life and of Nature. Life is stepping up more NOW to help you. (I am I)

Connecting with Archangel – Metatron and The Universal Oneness

Synchronising with Crystals –
Selenite, Labradorite, Hypersthene Labradorite

Before you gained awareness, it was taken for granted that life was pure luck and chance and that you grabbed and went with what appeared. We now know this to be not so true. You attract what you need by your energies, with your thoughts and emotions, intent, Karma, soul, mind-set and more.

A period of feeling stuck is now over.

(I am I). Sometimes you get blocked by beliefs, thoughts, words and worries; sometimes it's by life if timing and conditions are not correctly in place for what's needed. Remember you can't always see the whole picture and barely know the role you play in it. You know life has many stages that must be moved through for different reasons of personal development – whether physical, karmic or soul. You know also that things keep repeating until you grow beyond a need for them to happen or when you've learnt how not to attract.

The opportunities here are more on a soul level to allow you and your life to expand; to bring in some new energy; to give you another chance to add more to your repertoire of love, caring, compassion and service; to add more to the mixture of all you have gained and give out. (I am I)

Life is continual progression. If you stay as you are without changing a thing, not only does boredom set in but you waste opportunities for life and more living to occur, to bring in new memories, experiences, talents and strengths that will propel you beyond your own comfort zone and perhaps what you thought was obtainable.

This is also a chance for you to mix with new people and places. Life is asking that you share your energies, your wisdom and gifts to help others. Much growth obtained so far was purely for you; to get you back on track and life flowing. But what you have achieved cannot only stop there, like the ripples on a pond must keep going until momentum runs out. First life steps in to help you. Then you too have to share, to help as you too have been helped, not just for your own peace of mind and achievement, but because you too form a valuable link in the unfolding of the whole complete picture. Even if you think you know only very little, it can be seeds or much more to someone else knowing nothing at all of the things you have learnt on this level.

(I am I). Nothing is given to store up in a box within one soul. All is for reason, for purpose. You have been waiting for life to kick in to help you. What is needed will soon be here. In the meantime get ready, clear out excess clutter in home and mind to keep the route clear for insights, information and fresh opportunities. Remain ready, much as if treading water. (I am I)

Not all that comes along will be destined for you, so use your discernment; if it's not what you need or if you have grown beyond what comes up – it's alright to say no and wait for the next opportunity. These are a little like waiting for a bus. You wait for ages then many come all at once. Even then you must be selective. Some destinations are wrong. Some will be full or may go too far for too long, so again you must wait for the right one to appear to then take it. There will be no wrong choice – but routes will be varied and different.

(I am I). I know also what you came to achieve on soul level. I will place what is needed for the next phase of your journey in line with conscious thoughts and awareness. (I am I).

Affirmation – On a higher soul level – I am willing to explore something new.

PAIN

Pain can be physical or energetic. Both can feel strong.
Both will feel real. Both will pull you down
if you don't keep them within good control.

Connecting with Archangel – Raphael
and Your Personal Guardian

Synchronising with Crystals –
Blue Lace Agate, Rose Quartz, Red Jasper, Sugilite, Malachite

(I am I). I am positive. Love is positive. The energies of Nature are neutral until tuned into a negative or positive charge through attention, use or intent. Positive and negative are different polarities, like opposite ends of a magnet, like fire and water, both exist simultaneously but together the two will not mix. (I am I).

People handle pain very differently. Physical pain can engulf you completely until it's brought under control. There's usually a cause somewhere within the physical body (sometimes even caused by emotions and memory imprint) that once addressed becomes better or released.

(I am I) It often comes down to personal mind set. If you can rise above it, then pain can be easier to manage (once causes are correctly determined). If you let pain engulf you – you'll become it. If pain rules your kingdom, your whole outlook will reflect those limitations that appear to exist.

But the pain we speak of here today is pain on an emotional level, linked to past memories and hurts that won't fade, or present patterns and conditions taken personally, often imposed by other people/circumstances, that when they grip can take control until nothing else seemingly matters or exists.

Yet you have control of your life and your senses completely. Nothing and no one can hurt you unless on some level you let them. This acceptance is often subconscious; you can be so used to struggling, living and being that you forget other options exist. (I am I).

Emotional pain is more like a virus. It becomes all consuming, will sabotage at will and has no other purpose but to multiply itself, and will keep on doing so until somehow, sometime you realise. Pain is a negative. There is no such thing as a positive pain, unless in your mind you invent it or it's needed to slow you down to recuperate.

No one can feel what you feel ordinarily. Others may see you're not right from the outside but remember they won't always know why. When you get too down too often they'll think you're in a mood – even if inside you're bleeding for some love, kindness, understanding or compassion, on the outside no-one will know. And it's no use sending out signals or talking in riddles because these simply won't translate across. To those on the outside you'll just appear snappy or awkward and in yet another one of your moods.

Life is a mirror – you know that. All given out will just reflect back to make issues again more increased. If you send out sadness and pain – life (as the mirror) can only direct to you more of the same. If you're locked into depression, if you're fed up, down, sad or worried – again just the same reflects back. If you're in a relationship – or even when you think of yourself as you wish for more kindness and love or something other – think of the mirror. It will give you 'searching for kindness and love – or something other'.

Everyone around you is searching for the same love and happiness that you are. No one searches for what they feel they have already, so everyone is looking, including you, to find what is 'missing' outwardly in somebody else. But we all look and search the wrong way. You have it already – it's you! You are the love. You are kindness, compassion, understanding and everything else. You have to be these things yourself unconditionally for them to be mirrored back – without tags at no charge. You don't do what you do for payback – you do all you do because you can and because it makes you feel good. Life's mirror can then send back the same. If you search always for payback from life and others – life will reflect 'always searching for payback' – and that's too what you'll then see in others.

The whole of your life can be compared to a cake. When lost deep in pain it can feel like the whole complete thing as you break and so all crumbles down. But the common denominator is you – from the inside you felt you had broken (remember the mirror – how all you send out comes back much increased?.) In reality every aspect of yourself and your life is only one slice, a portion – not the whole thing. Learn to segregate into sections the areas that have become jumbled. Once this is done, all will be easier to manage. (My other books – And So It Begins.... Life Is Calling... Believe & Achieve and Divine Guidance – will greatly help here). Life will soon start to be very different.

(I am I). When your mood is in a negative, your next words, thoughts and actions will be also. Any help that is given by those working with you on levels Celestial or Physical won't be felt or have any effect because free will and negativity will have blocked all else out from inside – until you realise and come back into balance. (Remember that life is a mirror). (I am I)

You are the one who can turn this whole monster around by no longer giving it credence and therefore live substance. Put on your favourite music and jump about; dance out what's been bringing you down; step outside and take in some air, some deep, long, clear breaths and let go; open some windows; light some incense, sage the house, make some bread, tidy up, clear some space. Do all and anything you can to break free of the hold of the cycle, to add nothing more to it and then continue as though it doesn't exist. This will not make you a door mat – but will instead bring you back into your power. The mirror of life will always reflect more of the same.

Affirmation – I release all attachment to pain, anguish, stress – to step into my true highest self and my power.

REBIRTH

(I am I) Your essence is getting finer and brighter. Let the old fall away for the new. You are working your soul journey well. (I am I)

**Connecting with Archangel – Chamuel
and The Universal Oneness**

Synchronising with Crystals – Shiva Lingam, Opal, Malachite

It was not long ago that sages sat in solace and seclusion to gain enlightenment and a closer connection to God/Source/the Universal life force. It was good. It worked well.

But today that same connection, love and wisdom are needed in everyday life. It's whilst living amongst the people, doing all that should be done ordinarily that intervention and divine guidance are most needed.

You are part of this evolutionary process. All you have been through was necessary to get you to the point of understanding and awareness you have reached here today. NOW the real reason that you birthed can come in.

For over 2000 years and much more humanity on a physical level has been working to achieve love and peace. This has not always been as easy as it could have been given mentality, ideology and conditions unfolding/conflicting, so collectively this is as far as we've got.

We are much older than we realise for we've been here before, and at the end of each lifetime we reviewed it and promised to do better; but once again we must pass through the birth process where all higher knowledge of higher things is left behind, forgotten, to need again to be discovered from the present time frame and existence you are living.

All this to-ing and fro-ing is not helpful to life in relation to evolution and peace. It takes time to keep repeating the very same things, to get hardly further forward in the long run.

You have heard of ascension. You are ascending; your soul is getting finer, brighter, lighter and climbing to higher heights. What you're feeding back into life is purer, better.

Life in turn connects better with you.

To birth in peace all by ourselves on this physical earthly level is impossible. Again look at how we've faired in over 2000 years. This is as far as we've come. But from the higher realms of Heaven those working with us are also unable to birth peace alone. They are not here now in density, living physically. This is our time, with free will and our own conscious choice. If anyone or anything should intervene and overrule – the very structure of free will would negate.

In this time frame of today we are starting to ascend. We are accessing data that before now we would have 'died' first to then understand and see and gain; the problem there is that by that time our story would be over. Nothing more could then be done to fine-tune, alter, reshape or to negate.

To access this work right now allows us the freedom to review our lives in full whilst still physically living here; to counsel self and others; to become the higher version of the soul we know we are; to sweep and clear mistakes; to pay back into life and start afresh – from a heightened perspective; remembering it's by the grace of the Divine working with and through us now that we are able to do exactly this today, regardless of what's gone on before, of what we've done or who we think we are, we're given another chance to do things better, to re-align and to remember, to rise up ever higher, to re-shape and finally shine.

The lower levels of heaven are descending to meet with us. As we rise individually, collectively, the two levels of existence are blending, overlapping and are working in sync as One; in this way the real time magic can occur. Whatever we do will be much increased through the energy, love, efficiency and abilities of those working with us on levels celestial and spiritual. We can access their power and vision, higher wisdom, truths, insight and energy and blend it personally with our live connection to the present to ground and rebalance what is needed. Together and only together can we turn life and peace around.

This is soul work that you too birthed to achieve. It's why you've been through all you have, because from the understanding of knowing you've personally gained – you know exactly what needs help, mending, changing, rearranging or more love. You know where life is stuck and what should ideally occur to make it better.

Rebirth is not something ahead that you must 'die or pass over' to achieve. It's happening right here – right now – around and even to you as you finally open up to recognise/remember/see/receive.

(I am I). You are life itself, evolving, surviving, expressing, exploring in all connotations that exist. All and everything becomes part of Me. I am real. I am you. I am all you'll come to be and all that exists in totality.
(I am I)

Affirmation – I am all that I am and will be.

REFLECTION

(I am I). The past has no power beyond what you allow
and what you continue daily to feed it.
Nothing can be accessed or changed other than from
the pinpoint of NOW. (I am I).

Connecting with Archangel – Jeremiel
and Your Personal Guardian

Synchronising with Crystals –
Citrine, Amber, Zincite, Muscovite, Labradorite, Pearl

Almost nothing that has occurred was ever meant to harm. Very few things were meant to be personal. Life just happens in all ways that it does for everyone, to everyone, perhaps in different packages or in different order, but stuff is still stuff just the same. Who's to say one pain is larger than another, that grief and bad luck have a scale. Life is just life, not even bad or good because alone life knows nothing of that, it just is. But who and what then is its real driving factor?

Much you do in life is chosen in the moment as life unfolds without any more thought or attachment than that. Sometimes things are chosen and you won't remember or understand why; sometimes you go along with the flow; some things are for karmic clearance; or what's chosen is reaction instead of creation to bring in growth as well as understanding for later, so in hindsight you'll remember how easy it was to fall off track – before you judge another for their actions for something similar.

For whatever underlying reasons life happened or you chose things you did. There's little point in dragging the past along with you, wishing that things could be different or that you could be still there, because then you're keeping it going beyond where you should with the charge of live energy of now, placing on it false meanings and labels from memory, not necessarily from truths that occurred at the time. Should anything have been different – it would have been, because you always made the best choices possible from what you believed was available or you wanted. Would anyone deliberately choose a worse opposite – especially when there are repercussions?

If you altered even one tiny fragment of the past you would not be who you are at this moment. Your life would be different; you'd be like a different person, in a different place and surroundings entirely – and who's to say it would be much better? Of course it would be different, that's for sure, but better?

All choices you made came from what was occurring at that time in your life, your understanding, emotions, hormones, conditioning and wider programming. Mistakes made were really just that – mistakes, sometimes even whoppers, but look at what you then received back in terms of teachings and growth. Life's real gems and blessings are not always visible at first glance immediately; sometimes not even for years – if ever. They can only be measured at soul and karmic levels, but even then we might not see things entirely and may no longer be here to make changes.

Remember far more occurs out of view than we realise or know. Sometimes we do something for the benefit of another and then view it ourselves as a mistake.

(I am I) Believe you are lost and you will be. Think you are lonely or hard done by and that's exactly what you'll get back. Believe you are a bad person, a bad influence or victimised and life will reflect more as you create and compound that negating vibration – for no one will ever judge you more harshly than yourself.

Life needs for you to be able to look at the past like a set of old photographs. You've been there, done it and moved through. You don't need to keep bringing what's past and out of time along with you to remain active in the NOW time you are facing. Look back by all means: understand, squirm, recognise, love, laugh, learn, remember and let go. Create a NOW that's much better because of what you NOW know – not despite what you feel you are lacking. (I am I)

Creation needs you completely present and on par. Judge no-one by their past because you don't know the script of their story; you can't know what they've been through or why; what they needed to tick on their own soul agenda – or what they agreed to do or be to unleash the current gifts of another – perhaps even you. Whatever they'll carry will be theirs – not yours, so let go. And don't judge yourself too harshly either. Instead live now well. You won't see the whole picture until your life and time here are all done.

Look at the past. Know you've been there and accept it all happened. Not because you approve or condone it but because every aspect has made you worthwhile today.

> **Affirmation – All is divinely in tune as it should be – to bring me to where I am NOW.**

REJECTION

(I am I). Life is asking that you stop pushing. Pull back.
Conditions are not in tune with your needs.
(I am I)

**Connecting with Archangel – Chamuel
and Your Personal Guardian**

Synchronising with Crystals –
Smokey Quartz, Beryl, Magnesite, Rose Quartz

Love, laughter, contentment, bliss, peace and creativity – are all positive or neutral states of mind. When you experience any one of these you are happily in tune and flow with life and all is well. Rejection on the other hand is a negative. It's a product of the ego. Whether triggered by yourself or by others, it can be extremely powerful, hurtful, sometimes all consuming; your best option at the moment is to pull back into safety and wait for conditions to turn around, calm down or even change.

You can't always control life; can't stop people being people; can't stop what they'll do or say ordinarily. What you do have control over is how you take these things on board; whether you let them bring you down to affect your mood and outlook or you retract a little first and pull back into safety, to emerge fully later when the main storm has passed and all is clearer.

At the first sight of discord recognise what is occurring. Don't be like a wall that blocks the way and takes full brunt, but pay attention, notice the signs and signals arising inside yourself or sent by others; know the root cause and then retreat; allowing you to keep your power, integrity and inner calm intact; giving you the freedom to speak your truths at some point later more conducive to that input.

(I am I). At the onset of any turmoil – call for Me. I will always answer. I have the power to negate the largest problem – to make it less, therefore malleable for understanding, solution or correction. To stand your ground within full force will often make it worse and more destructive, especially if you stand

within your power. Even if you are correct this is not the time to say so. Wait until things calm down and a window opens up for you to work with – but again even then call on Me. (I am I)

Rejection usually means that someone has a wrong impression, that there is hurt, mistrust or disempowerment lurking somewhere. When you shine at your brightest others notice their darker shades; feeling less than really they are – fears, jealousy and stubbornness take centre stage – behaviours and attitudes can often change completely.

The truth is that whatever is occurring – it's more often based on lack, illusion and mistrust than higher vision. It's at times like these that help and healing must be called for.

Positive energy will be applied by those unseen working with you. Ask God/Source/the Universe for what is needed for yourself and for others to bring in peace and what's required to negate this; then step back, add nothing more; do something physical, completely different (housework, cooking, gardening, yoga, gym, go for a run or something else), do anything you can to shift the focus of your attention from the issue presenting and thereby release the building energy and tension; but be sure to ask the same for other parties involved – as it's as important for them as for you.

Life is like a cake. You only need a few ingredients for it to turn out well. If you keep on adding more or can't stop poking in the oven, you'll get a mess and make the clean-up harder too.

Let this go. Get on with something else worthwhile that needs your full attention. Do anything you can to not add more to what's occurring. Let life rebalance equally on everyone's behalf. When things have shifted later you'll get a chance to say your bit, but only from a point of love and kindness, from the bottom line of truth and what's productive and worthwhile – not from a place you've built up to fester in anger – to then let words uncontrollably rip.

Affirmation – Sometimes patience, understanding, love and a guiding gentle hand will work its magic far better than the need to be right in the moment...

RESISTANCE

(I am I). When resistance occurs it's a natural sign
to slow down; meaning life or situations need
more time or input to set things in place to
support this if all can go ahead. (I am I).

**Connecting with Archangel – Metatron
and Your Personal Guardian**

Synchronising with Crystals –
Lapis Lazuli, Zincite, Rhodocrosite, Beryl, Green Chlorite

All things in life have a time slot to begin, to peak and to end, as part of the natural order of life.

Earth is a complete working system within its own right. It works with precision to produce every need to sustain the entire living entity that we know as this planet itself. If humans were not here the whole matrix would continue. Earth doesn't need us in the way that we need it – but no one would exist here to love, know, measure, care or understand anything.

Every live system upon living earth has an equally precise working system all of its own to maintain and continue itself which then connect down to ever smaller and smaller systems, all working independently within their own right but supporting and functioning as though a team. Whether we look smaller or larger – even beyond earth into the solar system, all things work together in sync, connecting and effecting everything indivisibly, keeping balance and order and life as we know it to be.

Humanity seems to be the most random denominator of all that exists in this system. Yes there are comets and other phenomenon, but they come and go – not exist and continue in a manner that we do for all time.

(I am I) If all systems are balanced then it stands to reason that all has a time and a place and a function that adds to the whole to support or keep order maintained. But humanity does not slot into this bracket either. (I am I).

In the life of being human we create, explore and do all that we do. We often feel life owes or works around us. All that we are and all that we have we expect to always be there as though on tap; and most of the time it's OK as we've set up our systems to make sure things work as required; but sometimes life, conditions, situations or people need a little more time to adjust, more space and support to deliver or adapt.

Resistance is not always personal. Sometimes it relates back to life or to people needing more information, more of something that's relevant before what's occurring can continue or be released.

Sometimes a delay is a good thing. It allows for re-checks, to ensure right conditions are in place or being met; sometimes it allows for life itself to step in with something better that wasn't at first instantly available. If things are not right a negative vibration or connection will occur or be felt, regardless of where, for what reason, on what level as all systems conjoin somewhere – as One.

Resistance is not a definite no. It means pull back a little right now, sit tight and wait until conditions are better or more fully and firmly in place.

To jump over the edge before a time life is ready is to fall into nothing and fail. For now you must bend like the willow. This is no time to dig in your heels or to push against the grain of what's happening. Soften your view, lower your stance, ensure all's correctly in place; allow the behaviour, intentions and words of other people to wash over you like tepid water, while you come back to inner peace and just wait.

(I am I). Nothing can birth before conditions are ripe. Sometimes life just needs to catch up. Wait for a clear NOW to go signal. (I am I)

Affirmation – I trust all will be as it should be.

SECURITY

A time to ensure all is safe, secure and in place –
energetically as well as physically.

Connecting with Archangel – Metatron
and Your Personal Guardian

Synchronising with Crystals –
Emerald, Tourmaline, Hematite, Chrysophrase

(I am I). How often do you take time to think about safety, not on levels you can see, but energetically on levels invisible? Do you find that you sometimes feel vulnerable without understanding the cause or knowing why? (I am I)

You waited a long time to birth into your body that grants you your physical life here. But there are those who exist who would love to find themselves in your place, who relish opportunities to cause annoyance or worse given a chance.

(I am I) Not everything in life is kind or good. Many so revolt against goodness because of their own grossness that love, happiness, light and compassion to them seem unfathomable. (I am I).

Before birth you joined with a being of light who agreed to protect and look after your energetic self or light body, until you could do it yourself. This soul is your guardian, your own personal Angel, who works continually unseen to protect, guide and propel you towards your awakening – towards your soul's higher purpose and ascension. This is by no means an easy task to fulfil, because through your own use of free will you're often all over the place.

Automatic behaviour and straying daydream thought strands remove you consciously from what's happening in the present. Recreational states caused by substances that some take, excessive alcohol or caffeine, strong prescriptions and sleep deprivation can remove you from yourself temporarily, to physically weaken and then break down the aura – rendering it vulnerable and less able to function, a bit like the Earth's ozone layer.

Not only that, when you're in altered moods or mind states – souls no longer in the body are more able to come in closer to enjoy and share the effects of what you're doing, as when they were here they did too. Sometimes they get caught in your weakened aura/magnetic field and thereby enhance your behaviour, more usually in a negative, destructive, angry, crass, non-rational thinking manner. Through the intent of your own will, having deliberately chosen your actions, your angel is sometimes less able to prevent this indefinitely, at which point they have little alternative but to wait for you to notice or realise the changes in behaviour occurring; and because this is not ordinary every day conversation it can perhaps take a while before you do.

When you enter public places you're directly in contact with all types of people and therefore all types of energy. Much like a sponge you can pick up almost anything that's passing including pains that aren't yours... scary, dark or violent movies can leave you feeling open and again energetically vulnerable.

All this and much more your guardian/Angel must combat. That's before you even start to wake up and dabble in things angelic/celestial/spiritual that you are now seriously learning and using.

The original battle between good and evil, light and dark, positive and negative is real, not because God or evil has made it so, but because humanity did. We ourselves fell into the negative way back at the very beginning and so the whole process has had to play and work out...

The position you own in your body and time frame is precious because without it you can't exist here in the manner you presently enjoy.

(I am I) Would you deliberately leave your whole house wide open for all and sundry to walk through and use? When you understand the why better – you'll remember to ask for protection; when security is in place – no fear will exist – you'll feel safe, leaving your mind set and energy more relaxed and open to achieve and receive, create, love, explore and express. (I am I)

Take care of what's physical in practical ways that you should. Replace personal belongings mindfully back in their right place, so you'll remember where they are when they're needed. Ask God/Source/the Universe and your own guardian/Angel to protect you and your loved ones energetically. Place yourself, your home, friends and all others in huge balls of brilliant white light – to keep what's needed safely in place and as security to keep you from harm. Learn to do this automatically when you go out to nightclubs or parties, when you enter public places or work space; perhaps pay it forward and ask God/your angel to do it for you at times you might forget.

Doing these things yourself – or at least asking for them to occur regularly – will help you feel more secure, sleep better, relax and retain more of the life force you need on a day to day basis. Your Angel's job will be easier too.

Affirmation – I ask that I am always protected.

SELF ESTEEM

I am valued, valuable and necessary. I have purpose.

**Connecting with Archangel – Uriel
and The Universal Oneness**

Synchronising with Crystals –
Variscite, Topaz, Smithsonite, Danburite, Sunstone,
Citrine, Opal, Amazonite, Peridot

(I am I). For many lifetimes you've toiled to reach where you are – but you don't always see what has been achieved or how far you've come on soul level. There is no way to see the whole picture while living it physically... (I am I)

No one is perfect. All people have stuff in their closets that only they know about, which in hindsight could have been handled at those times it arose a little better.

(I am I) Who can live upon Earth for a total life span and not make mistakes here and there? Don't measure yourself by those incidents, but instead from what really stands out, from the good that you've done and from what can be achieved going forward. (I am I).

Self-esteem (or the lack of it) is something that grows. It stems from childhood, from loved ones, from experiences, exploits, supposition and friends – as cause and effect of emotional or physical intelligence, traumas, influences and gains converted into beliefs that you carry.

But things are now changing. You are reshaping and your confidence is growing... You know you have gifts born from all you have lived, seen and been through. How you process live data is unique to you too, for you see the bigger world from that angle.

Life has worked along with you for the whole of the time you've been here and even before. You have never been alone or forgotten. Opportunities arose at times most appropriate to stimulate and enhance whatever was needed for growth. Types of work you went into might not wholly define you but will instead just form part of your journey and again highlight growth.

When you're ready you'll reassess everything, to pick out the stars, the main aspects and threads, to help you bring in what you'd like to continue, achieve or produce.

(I am I) Nothing stands blocking your way. Where before you were unsure, held back or shy, you are learning how to stand tall, step forward and deal with what comes up more productively and to not take all that happens so personally. You have wisdom, truths and talents within you that others need also to grasp, to help them continue their own journey unfolding with ease. You will help as you too have been helped; understand where others have reached or are stuck – as you have already been there and moved on; as your soul has retained that information. (I am I)

Self-esteem comes from owning yourself and your life; from knowing your strengths, talents, pitfalls and warts – as well as what you've endured to overcome and achieve so successfully. Don't stand in the shadows awaiting life, people, recognition or rescue to come. What's in you even now to accomplish, to give back to life for the help it gave you to overcome and find the true you?

Affirmation – With greater confidence I exercise my full potential and my truth.

THE BOOK

(I am I). I AM – the total live record – from the first point of thought at Big Bang. (I am I)

Connecting with Archangel – Zadkiel and The Universal Oneness

Synchronising with Crystals –
Rainbow Fluorite, Clear Quartz, Selenite

(I am I). This book is more about your own record, a personal blueprint of your history and parts played as a contributing factor within the world system. As yet your own story's unfinished. What still waits to be recognised or added to complete the live script unfolding before the pages close again and nothing more can be changed until the next time you choose to re-birth? (I am I)

Nothing exists within the pages of your book until personally by love, choice, deed or acceptance you place it in there yourself, for you write your own story every day that you are alive. Nothing is written in stone; all probability and possibilities reside in the ether – waiting for you to connect, to choose from them yourself through attraction, free choice, association, intent and free will. You set all you can imagine and invent into live play continually.

Every day you wake up is a new page awaiting instruction and recognition. When you want to change direction you can. When you want to reinvent who you portray yourself to be, this you can. When you want new experiences, with new friends, new work or to establish a completely new outlook/lifestyle that you can be proud of, you can do all of these things and more very easily – step by step. Nothing can prevent what you want to achieve or become during this lifetime as long as you put in the effort.

(I am I). When your Earth life is over, retained within your soul, is all that through time you've accomplished. You'll see the overall picture of your own life playing out, but this time from a higher perspective of the total world view, the role that you played within the lives of family, friends, colleagues and strangers.

You'll discover whether you were an asset or a drain to Earth's own health and wellbeing and to the overall matrix of evolution still in play and continuing NOW, the chances and opportunities you missed, times you could have made better judgements, decisions, connections, positive changes and given higher hope/input to heal dramas and scenarios playing out. (I am I).

This book comes not only from a perspective of this life, not only from perspective of all lives you've lived, but also from a point of the history of all you've been and seen so far – as your soul has witnessed. And it doesn't end there. It's the record of the past in totality, your own past, the old ways of life and living having played out as far they could – before life itself could reach in to assist without undermining natural order, to deliver a long awaited awakening – rebirth/reboot/a higher more complete Divine understanding of all that's at stake here and what you are physically part of.

It's good that you grew to this level to receive and to know these things now, because you are one of the first still living here physically to do so, and you didn't need to die to receive it. There's still time to fine-tune, to recreate and redraw your real-time present day unfolding story; to revaluate the past from this higher perspective and to put into place what's needed now with insight, love, kindness and wisdom, to bridge the gap between the old and the new.

These are the things that along with your highest self only you can bring through.

You are ascending; blending with life celestial; together you are building/grounding the real Heaven on earth that prophets throughout the ages have predicted. Be thankful that you are here now to perform your part of that function.

(I am I). I am able to report this is true. (I am I)

Nothing of this nature can occur here on Earth until all realms combine to make One – so that is the meaning of your book.

> **Affirmation – I am consciously awakened, aware and creating.**

THE CHILD

(I am I). To enter the highest Celestial realms and to be closest to God – Souls evolve back into innocence, purity, goodness, love, wisdom, openness and light. (I am I)

Connecting with Archangel – Jeremiel and Your Personal Guardian

Synchronising with Crystals –
Amethyst, Rhodocrosite, Rose Quartz, Sugilite

Life is evolving. Earth is rebalancing. Humanity is ascending now en masse.

Every soul that is here now is born to 'lighten-up', to reduce the load that's carried, to raise personal vibration, to restructure, realign and blend more consciously closely with Heaven. The physical world is heavy. What we plough attention into can get weighty, draining, dense. If you are a high vibration soul it may be hard to function between the world's old structures falling, changing – and the new that's blending in.

Computers, tablets, smartphones, TV, series box sets, virtual games and more besides on level one. Fear, stress, worry, broken sleep and then low energy and self- esteem; tense relationships, commitments, financial burdens, world affairs and more uncertainty are on another. Even lifelong trusted back bone structures are surely crumbling away, leaving many feeling naked, vulnerable, unsure of what to do or expect next.

But now the good stuff.

Every once upon a while life on earth goes through a shake-up. This we are having now, collectively as much as individually within our own life; meaning we're able to bear the brunt the storms in the same boat all together, which takes the pressure off in times of pain and hardship. We 'know' it can't be 'our fault' because what's occurring is everywhere – so even though there's major turmoil, in a strange sense we can relax and bear what's happening – for in that same boat all together we feel safer.

Children are at their very best when they're free and happy, doing what they like to do when in play and fun. Their energies are vibrant, free and flowing well. They love surprises and adventure, meandering without the structure. What's unknown is fun to them, full of magic, wonder. With no expectations beyond what is – they seize the moment and go with it unencumbered.

Adults are more serious; life is heavy, denser. The rate at which we vibrate is therefore denser too. We think more deeply; speak, act and move in general at a slower pace and then relax with soothing pastimes to recuperate, so again we're still. We don't like shock or change and plan ahead into the future to fill up that space too, but lament when weeks are busy with little time left for enjoyment or adventure.

On a worldly scale, the deeper we reach into earth the ground gets harder, denser as all vibration slows. Towards the surface all is finer lighter, and we can use it more efficiently to sustain our many needs.

Adults become aligned with denser earth the less they move and do, the more they stress and worry, the more they cling to what they build and have, the more they fear they'll lose, the more they dislike change. Children by comparison are much lighter. Sure they don't have all the burdens yet that later they will get, but in their world they too have loads to carry – with work to do, learn, use and move through. On the whole they stay much lighter so they align with finer energies that sustain and keep them buoyant, vibrant longer. Creativity and life flows freely, they are happy.

It's known the realms of Heaven consist of finer substance, like ice would be to steam and steam to gas. To be childlike once again is to lighten up, to be open and carefree; not from the realms of throwing what is now in place and necessary away to start again, but from a high perspective of releasing what is stale and heavy, no longer working well and out of tune – back out to life, back to God/Source/the Universe, to recycle and readjust on our behalf – to let help in so life can flow where things were blocked. Remember much of what is dealt with here links in with thought and energy and old baggage.

(I am I) Instead of forcing things to fit – step back and reassess. When you release your hold on life even just a bit, I can remove what's stale and stagnant to unblock the system for creativity and movement to flow in... (I am I)

Affirmation – Today there's room to play and to enjoy life.

THE CLIFF

(I am I). Every day holds something that when grasped
will serve to take you further forward.
(I am I)

**Connecting with Archangel – Haniel
and The Universal Oneness**

Synchronising with Crystals –
Connemara Marble, Prehnite, Garnet, Zeolite,
Apophyllite, Sunstone, Malachite, Magnesite, Ruby

(I am I). No-one is made to stagnate. From birth until death and even beyond the soul is unlimited. Nothing will ever prevent this – except you – and how you choose to process your life. (I am I).

Nothing is written within your soul destiny that you cannot handle or grow from. No-one's live path is easier than another's for all contain reason and purpose.

(I am I). Now is a time for you to be brave, to take steady steps to birth in a new future that beckons – but with love, higher purpose and kindness, moving only in terms of highest good and intention. (I am I).

This is a time to redraw your present life, your real-time live picture, presentation and boundaries; what you want, need and wish for; what you will or will no longer accept; what you'll tolerate or want to birth in.

From a perspective of growth and rebirth you have put much of your Karma to bed. Everything you have lived through was necessary. Much contained paybacks as well as hidden gifts that you needed to collect or work through to propel you towards this next level.

Don't be tempted to change too much too fast. This is more about the realisation that life has become stagnant or stale, like a pair of old slippers completely worn through, that might still be loved but their purpose and best usage have passed.

(I am I) I have already begun to bring in new life, movement and purpose which you have now felt for a while. It's time to turn things around for the better – not to throw things away – but to grow forward and up beyond the place life is stuck, to let love, joy, bliss and happiness in. (I am I).

Know you will not fail in your endeavours. First the soul stirs, ideas form and inspiration flows in. Next you will put into place exactly what's needed to support the next steps you will take, the difference being here that you're no longer alone but acting with and on behalf of greater good with God/Source/the Universe and those working along with you unseen.

Life is kick–starting again, not from the very beginning but with the benefit of all you have gained to this point as you recognise the real potential in 'you'.

(I am I). Every day is a gift to be lived in its own right. Enjoy where you are and be happy – for the best to come in as it should. (I am I)

Affirmation – I am ready to take useful steps.

TRANSFORMATION

Miracles; Magic; Movement; Metamorphosis;
Monumental Creativity; Awakening and New Awareness
coming in...

Connecting with Archangel – Uriel
and The Universal Oneness

Synchronising with Crystals –
Tiger's Eye, Moonstone, Opal, Scolecite, Charoite, Malachite, Herkimer Diamond, Larimar

Every soul will reach this pinnacle at some stage within its journey of existence. You have reached it now as the outcome, the culmination of lives lived; of attainment; of Karma cleared and moved beyond; of soul awakening and progression; of knowledge gained and put to use; of realisation, understanding, awareness and right action put in place.

Life is living through you actively – through the actions, thoughts, intent and purpose of your soul.

You are working/blending with the laws of pure creation. Even now as you read these words you can feel these truths within. Nothing blocks the way ahead – you're firmly on the path you came to tread.

Every word and thought you have is now important. All will take you forward or hold you back, lift you higher or keep you down – the choice is yours; so remain aware and recognise the subtleties of what emerges, how and when. Nothing will prevent this natural occurrence, much like a chain reaction that stems from deep within...

(I am I) Nothing destined to be yours will be missed. All will come about in order and to plan. You have lived your own part well to reach this very point – but life will never stop – this signifies another higher level of awareness and attainment opening up for more discovery, personal development and fine tuning/soul growth.

Light is coursing through you. New information and understanding is flooding in.

You have opened up again for more expansion and higher purpose to pour in.

Work your life force well. Recognise what holds you back – and release it up to Me in times and ways appropriate – for you really do live life and work creation on life's behalf. (I am I)

Affirmation – I Am.

UNCONDITIONAL LOVE

Unrestricted; Absolute; Unreserved; Accepting;
Understanding; Non Judgemental; Eternal...

Connecting with Archangel – Jeremiel
and Your Personal Guardian

Synchronising with Crystals –
Rose Quartz, Amazonite, Morganite

Every person wants to love and be loved. Nothing is more important.

(I am I). You were born of love; you were made from love; but do you realise that love is the bond that connects to all of life – even when you believe it's not present? (I am I).

Everyone tries to find love by searching outside of themselves – in loved ones, family, strangers, wider life and friends. But how often do you feel love come back? From a very early age you were taught that love was conditional; that it had to be earned; that it looked and presented in certain ways; that you had to deserve it, even drive, steal and win it. People either fit your expectations or they don't. You fit into theirs – or you don't. When you don't fit you will feel it so again you'll try harder to step up, to re–shape or to please, to try to make fit what you thought wrong or broken or just missing by standards in place everywhere.

Set conditions exist all around you – at home and at work and in life. But who gets to set them? Who says they are right? Who feels the weight that you carry as you work hard to make the love that you feel and need fit? And doesn't love carry different meanings for everyone?

(I am I). More love exists within you as well as without than you realise. All things stem from it. Everything you are, have been and will be stems from it also – even before you were physically born. Every decision and choice that you 'will' into being stems from the same conscious/subconscious place

of something you thought 'you'd love to happen' – so by the grace of creation it does... (I am I)

Yet unconditional love means unconditional. No tags. It means that you give without expecting back. (Not that you expect nothing back or you'll get nothing back because of life's mirror, but it means no labels, no surplus thoughts or underlying deeper expectations of tally or returns of any kind, that love will flow in and flow out and just be).
You carry no record of what's gone on before, how, where, when and why; you give freely of what you have and what you are because you want to, because you can – when you can, because that's who you are and what you do, not always physically, materialistically from your own pocket, but energetically, spiritually, on a soul to soul level all of the time, without expectation, exception or prompt. But to be able to do all of this you must accept unconditionally all aspects of your own self, past and present. Why would you not when you've given your very best, when decisions taken were OK at the time or you would not have made those decisions, when mistakes that you made were just that – mistakes?

Know the people around you don't live to be mean, even if sometimes they may want you to think so. They don't make it their aim to shoot arrows and hurt and are often just hurting themselves – or tired or down, sometimes thoughtless, deflecting. They may be stuck in a rut on their own journey's path, with their outlook of life being difficult, unfair or repressed, very different from expectations, live effort or dreams they once had or still carry. Sometimes further influences overrule them. You on the other hand are lucky. You are waking up to the real essence of love and life and this understanding goes a very long way.

(I am I). The purpose of every live journey over and over again (apart from the obvious) is to climb ever closer towards purity, towards the original essence that was life at the start.

Every soul forever links with Myself – no matter whom.

To believe you are separate and alone, that this connection We share is conditional – is false. To believe you must prove your worth to be loved, that I judge you with anger and ego – is false. To believe that life is a school with tasks you must pass to evolve and again prove your worth – is equally false, because each of these things are conditional; their presence would imply conditions attached to My own love and attachment with you. Instead you do all that you do and have done for the sake of fine tuning, for the sake of your own soul, further growth and development, to karmically undo what has been done before, if not by yourself – then by others.

Unconditional is My attachment. Unconditional My love and all provided through time, even the chance to come back to do better, to become more than you perhaps know you are.

Now say again that your love, your outlook and attachments are unconditional. (I am I)

To love unconditionally means that you really understand, see, feel and know other souls; that you realise that each one is separate; that each is searching to find where it is they belong, their best fit; each is searching to find their way home.

Nothing in life is meant to be personal, to cause you anguish and pain, but if you feel that it is – on some level you believe or have accepted it is so; you have given away personal power and have felt that to gain the love you feel you deserve – conditions must be recognised and met.

No one owns you. No one owes you.You owe and own no one either. All souls are in the same boat. All occurs because someone somewhere deemed it so. To receive love you must be love. Unconditional love first stems
from inside.

Affirmation – I AM UNBIASED LOVE UNCONDITIONAL.

Essential Prayers of World Religions

Buddhism: The Refuge Prayer
Christianity: The Lord's Prayer
Islam: The Fatiha
Hinduism: The Gayatri Mantra
Judaism: The Shema

Buddhism: The Refuge Prayer
Buddham saranam gacchami
I go to the Buddha for refuge.
Dhammam saranam gacchami
I go to the Dhamma for refuge.
Sangham saranam gacchami
I go to the Sangha for refuge.

Christianity: The Lord's Prayer
Origin: The gospel of Matthew, chapter 6
Our Father, who art in heaven,
Hallowed be thy name.
Thy kingdom come,
Thy will be done,
on earth as it is in heaven.
Give us this day our daily bread
And forgive us our trespasses,
as we forgive those who trespass against us.
And lead us not into temptation,
but deliver us from evil.
For thine is the kingdom, the power,
and the glory, for ever and ever.
Amen.

Islam: The Fatiha

Origin: The opening words of the Qur'an
In the name of Allah, Most gracious, Most merciful
Praise be to Allah, the Cherisher and Sustainer of the
Worlds
Most gracious, Most Merciful.
Master of the Day of Judgement
Thee do we worship, and Thine aid we seek
Show us the straight way
The way of those on whom Thou has bestowed thy Grace,
those whose portion
Is not wrath, and who do not go astray.

Hinduism: The Gayatri Mantra

Origin: The Vedas
Oh Creator of the Universe, may we receive thy supreme
sin-destroying light. May thou guide our intellect in the
right direction.

Judaism: The Shema

Origin: The book of Deuteronomy, chapter 6
Hear, Israel, the Lord is our God, the Lord is One.
Blessed be the Name of His glorious kingdom for ever
and ever
And you shall love the Lord your God with all your heart
and with all your soul and with all your might.
And these words that I command you today shall be in
your heart.
And you shall teach them diligently to your children, and
you shall speak of them when you sit at home, and when
you walk along the way, and when you lie down and when
you rise up.

And you shall bind them as a sign on your hand, and they shall be for frontlets between your eyes.
And you shall write them on the doorposts of your house and on your gates.

The Divine Feminine/Goddess Prayer

Hail Mary,
Full of Grace,
The Lord is with Thee.
Blessed art Thou amongst women,
And Blessed is the fruit of thy womb Jesus.
Holy Mary,
Mother of God,
Please pray for us,
Now and at the hour of our death,
Amen.

This is not given as a religious recitation, but more as an example of connection to the archetypical Divine Feminine, instead of connecting just to the Divine Male of the Lord's Prayer alone.

All pathways have their own version. Find and know yours. Use it.

For how can the help you need be given to its highest capacity if you don't connect to the top of the mountain – or the top of the tree – to the Oneness we're completely part of?

When you connect to the highest (religious connotations placed aside – working on totally the physical – on how you connect to, interact and communicate with life itself) – you open yourself up to ALL help available instead of limiting yourself and that help to just a few levels.

Remember you don't know the whole picture – only the part that you have lived and know – but even then, are we as sure of that labelling as we should be?

If we were right – wouldn't we all be a lot happier and more forward – wouldn't the world be more united and at peace - even now?

Using both the feminine and masculine together is the equivalent of the whole yin and yang. Masculine being the male strength, the backbone and provider – Feminine being the softer, gentle strength – but equally as powerful; the womb and caring nurturer; the side of ourselves that can make anything work from the basis of what we already know and have to the sticking plaster that blinds and holds the whole thing together.

Meaning Of The Radha Govind Samiti – Daily Prayer

I bow down to my gurudev's lotus feet again and again.

"Know the guru to be Myself (God). Never think unfavorably about Him. Do not use your material mind to comprehend the guru's Divine actions, for all forms of God dwell within Him." (Bhagvatam)

O my Divine Beloved! O supreme Lord Krishna! I have been suffering from countless sorrows as a result of having ignored You since beginningless time. Committing sins lifetime after lifetime has made my heart so impure that in spite of having learnt from Your loving saints that You are waiting for me with open arms to embrace me and benevolent eyes to grace me, I still fail to surrender to You.

O shelter of the shelterless! It is impossible to know You without Your grace in such a situation.

O causelessly-merciful Shri Krishna! O redeemer of sinful souls! Make me Yours with a glance of Your causeless grace.

O ocean of mercy! I have no desire for earthly or celestial pleasures, nor do I seek liberation. My only desire is to love You unselfishly.

O my lord! Keeping Your reputation in mind, do not disappoint this fallen soul.

O Treasure of my life! I have suffered enough. Now I have come to realise that life devoid of Your love is more frightening than death itself.

Therefore, I beg of You again and again:

Grant me alms of Your love. Grant me alms of Your love. Grant me alms of Your love.

Sikh - Ardās Prayer

Ek Ong Kaar Waheguru Ji Ki Fateh
There is one God. All Victory belongs to God.

Siri Bhagauti Ji Sahai
May the dynamic power of God help us.

Var Siri Bhagauti Ji Ki Paatshahi Dasveen
The Vaar (poetic verse) of Sri Bhagauti, composed by the
Tenth King.

Pritham Bhagauti Simmar Kai Gur Nanak Laeen Dhiae
Having first involved the dynamic power of God, call on Guru
Nanak.

Phir Angad Gur Te Amardas Ramdasai Hoieen Sahai
Then on Angad Guru, Amar Das and Ram Das, may they ever
protect us.

Arjan Hargobind Non Simrau Siri Har Rai
Then call on Arjan, and Hargobind, holy Har Rai.

Siri Harkrishan Dhiaeeai jis Dithe Sabh Dukh Jaie
Remember Holy Har Krishan, whose sight dispels all
sorrows.

*Teg Bahadar Simriye Ghar Nau Nidh Awai Dhaai. Sabh
Thaaeen Hoi Sahai*
Then remember Teg Bahadur by whose remembrance the
nine treasures come hurrying to one's home. Be ever with
us, O Masters.

*Daswan Patshah Siri Guru Gobind Singh Sahib Ji, Sabh
Thaaeen Hoai Sahai*
May the tenth king, Guru Gobind Singh, be ever on
our side.

*Dasan Patshahian Di Jot Siri Guru Granth Sahib Ji De Path
Didar Da Dheyan Dhar Ke Bolo Waheguru!*
Let us now turn our thoughts to the teachings of Guru Granth
Sahib, the visible embodiment of the ten Gurus and utter, O
Khalsa Ji, Vaheguru! (glory be to God).

*Panj Piarian, Chohan Sahibzadian, Chahlian Muktian,
Hathian, Jappian, Tapian, Jinhan Nam Jappia Wand Chhakia
Deg Chalai Teg Wahi Dekh Ke Undith Keetaa Tinnha Piarian
Sachiarian Di Kamaaee Da Dhiaan Dhar Ke Khalsa Ji Bolo Ji
Waheguru!*

The five Beloved Ones, the four Sahibzaade (sons of the tenth
Master), the forty emancipated ones, the martyrs, the true
disciples, the contemplators of God, and those who remained
steadfast on the path of Dharma, remember their glorious
deeds and utter O Khalsa Ji, Vaheguru.

*Jinahan Singhan Singhanian Ne Dharam Hait Sees Ditte,
Band Band Katae, Khoprian Luhaian, Charkhian Te Charhe,
Aarian Nal Chiraae Gae, Gurdwarian Di Seva Laee Kurbanian
Kithian, Dharam Naheen Hariaa, Sikhi Kesan Suasan Naal
Nibhahee, Tinnhaan Dee Kamaaee Da Dhiaan Dhar Ke Khalsa
Ji! Bolo Ji Waheguru!*

Those who dwelled on God's Name, shared their honest
earnings with others, wielded sword in battlefield,
distributed food in companionship, offered their heads at

the altar of Dharma, were cut up limb by limb, skinned alive, boiled or sawn alive, but did not utter a sigh nor faltered in their faith, kept the sanctity of their hair until their last breath, sacrificed their lives for the sanctity of Gurdwaras; remember their glorious deeds and utter O Khalsa Ji, Vaheguru!.

Panjan Takhtan Sarbatt Gurduaarian Da Dhiaan Dhar Ke Bolo Ji Waheguru!

Turn your thoughts to the five Takhats (seats of Sikh authority) and all the Gurdwaras and utter O Khalsa, Vaheguru!

Prithmen Sarbatt Khalsa JiKi Ardaas Hai Ji, Sarbatt Khalsa Ji Ko Waheguru Waheguru Waheguru Chitt Aawai, Chitt Aawan Kaa Sadkaa Sarab Sukh Howai. Jahaan Jahaan Khalsa Ji Sahib Tahaan Tahaan Rachhiaa Riaayat, Deg Teg Fateh, Birdd Kee Paij, Panth Ki Jeet, Siri Saheb Ji Sahaae, Khalsa Ji Ke, Bol Baale, Bolo Ji Waheguru!

First, there is supplication for all the Khalsa Panth. May the Lord bestow upon His Khalsa the gift of His remembrance, Vaheguru, Vaheguru,Vaheguru, and may the merit of this remembrance be happiness of all kinds. O God, wherever are the members of Khalsa, extend Your protection and mercy on them; let the Panth be ever victorious, let the sword be ever our protector. May the order of the Khalsa achieve ever-expanding progress and supremacy. Utter O Khalsa, Vaheguru!.

Sikhaan Noon Sikhi Daan, Kes Daan Rehitt Daan, Bibaik Daan, Visah Daan, Bharosa Daan, Danaan Sir Daan Naam Daan, Siri

Amritsar Ji De Ishnaan, Chowkian, Jhande, Bunge, Jugo Jug Attal Dharam Ka Jaikaar Bolo Ji Waheguru!

May God grant to the Sikhs, the gift of faith, the gift of uncut hair, the Keshas, the gift of discipline, the gift of spiritual discrimination, the gift of mutual trust, the gift of self confidence and the supreme gift of all the gifts, the communion with Vaheguru, the Name, and the gift of bathing in Amritsar.

May the administrative centres, banners, the cantonments of Khalsa ever remain inviolate. May the cause of truth and justice prevail everywhere at all times, utter O Khalsa, Vaheguru!.

Sikhan Daa Man Neevan, Matt Uchee. Matt Daa Rakha Aap Waheguru!
May the minds of Sikhs remain humble, and their wisdom exalted. Vaheguru! You are the protector of wisdom.

He Akaal Purkh Aapne Panth De Sadaa Sahaaee Dataar Jeeo, Siri Nankaana Sahib Te Hor Gurduaarian Gurdhaman De Jinhan Ton Panth Noon Vichhoria Giaa Hai, Khulhe Darshan Deedaar Te Sewaa Sambhaal Daa Daan Khalsa Ji Noon Bakhsho
Almighty Lord! Our helper and protector ever, restore to us the right and privilege of unhindered and free service and access to Nankana Sahib and other centers of Sikh religion from which we have been separated.

He Nimanian De Maan, Nitaniaan De Taan, Niotiaan Di Ot, Sachhe Pittaa Waheguru, Aap De Hazoor .... Dee Ardaas Hai Jee
God, the Helper of the helpless, the Strength of the weak, the Supporter of the fallen, the true father of all, (here the

specific purpose and the occasion for the supplication is stated by the person leading in the supplication and the blessings and aid of God are beseeched)

Akhar Wadhaa Ghaata Bhul Chukk Maaf Karnee. Sarbatt De Kaaraj Raas Karne. Saiee Piaare Mail Jinhaan Miliaan Tera Naam Chitt Aawe.

Forgive us O Lord, all our faults, extend Your helping hand to everyone. Grant us the company of those who may help keep Your Name fresh in our hearts.

Nanak Naam Charhdi Kalaa, Tere Bhane Sarbatt Daa Bhalaa.
Through Satguru Nanak, may Your Name be exalted and may all of mankind prosper according to your Will

Waheguru Ji Ka Khalsa, Waheguru Ji Ki Fateh.
The Khalsa belongs to God and to Him belongs the victory.

Sikh - Prayer Meaning

The Ardās is said as a reflection on everything it took for the Divine to create the pure Shabad Guru on earth and to remember all that the Sikh endured to protect it and ensure it landed in the hands of the future generation.

It encompasses many Sikh and Humanistic values, such as peace and understanding, as well as faith and perseverance.

Ardas is a unique Sikh prayer that was not written by the Gurus and cannot be found in the Guru Granth Sahib Ji (the holy book of the Sikhs).

Ardas is known to be changing and evolving prayer which is recited by an individual in accordance to his/her feelings, accomplishments and state of mind.
Therefore, the purpose of this prayer is to appeal to Waheguru (the supreme being) for protection, care and welfare of the mankind, while thanking Him for everything he has provided us with.

Ardas reflects upon Guru given Gurbani (prayers), appreciates the Sikh martyrs, preserves Humanistic values and peace, and cultivates faith. Ardas also provokes positive human emotions such as Nimrata (Humility), Daya (Compassion), Chardi Kala (fearlessness; in high spiritual state of mind). It encourages one to become a better Sikh and also a better human being by linking the minds to those of the "pure and brave ones" from history.

A sense of community and the betterment of the society (sarbat da bhala) are the key components of Ardas. Ardas is divided into three sections. First section remembers all the ten gurus and their legacies to the Sikh religion. Second section discusses the sacrifices made by brave and spiritual leaders of the Sikh history and conspires a Sikh to be like them and protect others from the unjust world and oneself from worldly vices. The third section allows a Sikh to appeal for any specific wants/needs and for any sort of forgiveness and further guidance. As mentioned before, this prayer ends with the ultimate appeal for the prosperity of humanity.

Muslim Prayer

In the name of Allah Most Gracious most Merciful.
Praise be to Allah the Cherisher and Sustainer of the Worlds.
Most Gracious Most Merciful Master of the Day of Judgement
It is you we worship and serve and it is you we seek help
from
Show us the straight way
The way of those upon who You bestowed Your Grace, not
those upon whom is anger, nor those who go astray.

or

The Fatiha
in the name of Allah
The Merciful, The Compassionate
Praise be to Allah
The Merciful The Compassionate
The Ruler of the Day of Judgement

You alone we serve
From you alone we seek our help
Lead us on the straight path
The path of those
Whom you have given grace,
Not on the path
of those upon whom your wrath resets
Nor on the path of the lost.

The Fatiha means 'The Opening' or 'The Opening of the
Fortress' because it is positioned before all the other suras
in the Quran. It is considered to be directly inspired by
Allah and contains the words spoken by Muhammed 1,350

years ago. Since that time, this prayer has been repeated by countless Muslim worshippers.

Sikh Prayer

MOOL MANTAR

EK OU – AN – KAAR - There is one God
SATNAAM - His name is true
KARTA PURKH - He is the Creator
NIRBHAU - He is without fear
NIRVAIR - He is without hate
AKAAL MOORAT - He is timeless, without form
AJUNI - He is beyond Birth and Death
SAIBHANG - He is self-existent
GURPRASAAD - He is realised by the true Gurus Grace
JAP - Meditate on his name
AAD SACH - He was true in the timeless beginning
JUGAAD SACH - He was true through the ages
HAI BHI SACH - He is true now
NANAK HOSI BHI SACH – Says Nanak, He
(GOD) will evermore be true...

Sufi – Morning Prayer

Saum
Praise be to Thee, Most Supreme God, Omnipotent, Omnipresent, All-pervading, the Only Being. Take us in Thy Parental Arms, raise us from the denseness of the earth. Thy

Beauty do we worship, to Thee do we give willing surrender, Most Merciful and Compassionate God, the Idealised Lord of the whole humanity. Thee only do we worship; and towards Thee alone we aspire. Open our hearts towards Thy Beauty, Illuminate our souls with Divine Light, O Thou, the Perfection of Love, Harmony and Beauty!

All-powerful Creator, Sustainer, Judge and Forgiver of our shortcomings, Lord God of the East and of the West, of the worlds above and below, and of the seen and unseen beings, pour upon us Thy Love and Thy Light, give sustenance to our bodies, hearts and souls, use us for the purpose that Thy Wisdom chooseth, and guide us on the path of Thine Own Goodness.

Draw us closer to Thee every moment of our life, until in us be reflected Thy Grace, Thy Glory, Thy Wisdom, Thy Joy and Thy Peace.
Amen.

Sufi – Prayer for Peace

Send Thy peace O Lord,
which is perfect and everlasting, that our
souls may radiate peace.
Send Thy peace O Lord,
that we may think, act and speak harmoniously.
Send Thy peace O Lord,
that we may be contented and thankful
for Thy bountiful gifts.
Send Thy peace O Lord,

that amidst our worldly strife, we may
enjoy Thy bliss.

Send Thy peace O Lord,
that we may endure all, tolerate all,
in the thought of Thy grace and mercy.
Send Thy peace O Lord,
that our lives may become a Divine vision
and in Thy light, all darkness may vanish.
Send Thy peace O Lord,
our Father and Mother, that we
Thy children on Earth may all unite in one family.
Amen.

Also by Stephanie J. King

And So It Begins
You have more power over life than you realise

This is the first book written in a series destined to rebuild the hopes and happiness of man, who has thought himself unworthy and abandoned for far too long. Man (being the universal word for humanity, for 'mankind'. Not placing the male gender over or above the female. All are equal) is connected to the true source of life, to the source of the planet itself. He has never been anything other.

Man was born to live the life that is here now. This is his heritage, not his punishment. Man was meant to be happy, living his choices, not downtrodden and depressed.

And So It Begins mirrors aspects of character that rarely get considered. It helps unburden clutter, blindly passed down through generations, to gently reseat the deepest foundations. The time that each person has left and how he chooses to use it is the key to his future, and his future begins here – physically and spiritually 'now'. This is his legacy.

(I am I) How many people recognise my hand in life? How many understand that I know their every thought, wish and movement? How many realise I am not the vengeful ruling force they think me to be? How many wish for love and recognition but do not yet realise it is already within – waiting to be unlocked and fully lived? (I am I)

And So It Begins will take you by the hand and lead you forward in a way that is safe and realistic to be beneficial from the very first time that you use it. Every soul alive is born with a life agenda – chosen by Him and higher beings – for his own soul's improvement. Each is on a journey of awakening and discovery. Each is placed in life where they can best achieve what needs to be accomplished and experienced.

Every soul, therefore every life, links directly to earth, to source, to the Universal consciousness itself. *And So It Begins* opens windows and doors to new insights and understanding that you may not have realised existed. Like an oracle/truth-mirror/real-time life guide, it will quickly highlight your soul purpose and life agenda. You'll know exactly who you are, what you're part of, what's going on with others and life around you, what you're able to achieve and contribute, where and why things get stuck as well as ways you can effortlessly change this. You'll view differently past and present; your Karma, talents, gifts and strengths, how others push your buttons and why you react – to stop repeating what you no longer need.

From teenager to elderly this book is already helping thousands to reassess what they've known, to rekindle dreams and goals, to turn life around and be happy. It highlights the negativities playing out in the present - to give you more choice and actually spins things around for the better. Read it as a book or dip into its pages (perfect for busy lifestyles), you'll actually feel yourself interacting with higher levels, with source, with your own spirit guardian/Angel/guide and with life – as if in direct conversation with a personal friend on a soul to soul level.

Empowered and completely in tune with where you are, you'll breeze through all aspects of life/love/work/family/ home and move forward with ease, clearing clutter and blockages accumulated through generations and the years that you've personally been here – but make no mistake – this is not like any other book you have previously read for self-development. *And So It Begins* will make a difference in your life and outlook right from the start. You'll feel healthier and happier with renewed energy and confidence, positivity, focus and life zest.

This book is perfect for the already developed mind as well as for the beginner.

Helping you to also help others, you'll become a light worker – for what you give out will always come back. In this manner you'll help life heal itself.

(I am I) The life force that is yours is unique. No one else can fill your shoes. No one else has had your same life experience. I need you to come back consciously to truths that wait here for you - to help ease your life 'now' and help you grow. (I am I)

And So It Begins can be used many times daily for up to the minute guidance that's completely in tune with what's happening around and about you, and as you receive this information – life will immediately respond in accordance. The help you need is here - the rest is up to you.

Life is Calling
How to Manifest Your Life Plan

Are you aware that you're living a live real-time soul journey and that your limited time span here contains targets, purpose and goals? That you have talents, strengths and tasks to accomplish and contribute? That you were born with a pre-chosen life agenda of your own? That you've lived on earth before? That you create your own reality and that daily life needs and takes instructions straight from you? Do you know you connect to earth's own creative, thinking mind and that everything about you interacts?

Each day is a new day. It is another chance to create, to make a difference, to redraw and redefine who you are and what you do. How you live, interact and connect with daily life means everything – for all achievements you'll take with you, back to the realms of spirit – as your contribution and offering to life, to physicality and to time.

Written like a deck of cards (with over 380 entries) but in an easy to manage book form, *Life is Calling* was channelled by spirit as a direct 'soul to soul' interchange. It's a link to advice for you from your own guardian/Angel/guide in a down to earth way that completely connects and relates to where you are. It will mirror everything as it highlights information that will prove relevant from the very first time that you use it.

Nothing happens by chance. You know everything about yourself, your thoughts, situations, history and events. You know what you believe in. Each time you pick it up *Life is Calling* will correspond to now and be precise in the guidance, words and knowledge being given. It will completely turn around, balance and correct many things that you both consciously and subconsciously do - so you can choose and re-choose as you go along, depending on what's playing out.

Life is Calling will help you manifest your own life plan step by step – and before long you will know exactly what that is and where you're heading. Labelled a phenomenon, this incredible interactive book will take you by the hand and deliver specific, tailored guidance at the precise time and place you need it most. It can be surprising to realise how much you matter and that someone, something, somewhere, knows you better than you even know yourself, better than your own mother, loved ones, family and friends do – for your guardian has always been with you – never judging, just helping and silently waiting for you to notice. Perfect for busy lifestyles, this powerful guide book will help you to change much for the better, as you access higher truths and information that are with you.

Link and work directly with life's own creative forces. Interact with source – as if being taken by the hand – so pure data, insights, inspiration, hunches and extrasensory information can filter through. Increase performance, optimise results, and reach targets and personal short and long term life goals easily, without an increase in effort from you – through renewed understanding and insight. Love, work, family and home – all results will be immediate and immense. This book has the potential to enhance the rest of your life – for the rest of the time frame that you live here.

Life Is Calling Concise Pocket/Handbag Version

Due to popular demand - *Life is Calling* is also now available in an abridged pocket/handbag size version. Many people love our book so much that nearly 200 entries 'specifically chosen by spirit' form this book – in a small easy to travel fashion size to see you through the day at random times.

Divine Guidance
The answers you need to make miracles

We physically live the miracle of life on this living, breathing, thriving planet every day. We have free choice and free will. We have the ability to love and grow; to move in any direction and to climb the highest heights that we can dare. Yet how often are we free to feel happy?

Divine Guidance is designed to work with you in the unfolding drama of your life story – in all ways unique and connected to you. It links to higher conscious mind through your own intelligence, through your energetic life force and higher self, linking with and through your guardian straight to Source/God/Earth/the Universal source of life that links to all. This book will take you by the hand to steer you through whatever is occurring to lead you forward, supporting, advising, to help you achieve the highest outcome available at any moment.

Miracles are a natural part of daily life – we just don't notice. According to your wants and needs life is trying to unfold in your best interest. But circumstances, thoughts, doubts, fears, emotions and many more things get in the way. Not all you hear, see, feel or know is beneficial...

What possibilities would await if you could navigate the life you live more effectively, staying one step ahead of others and of change? What if you always had a solution for the many challenges you face – to ease your journey? Do you want the best from what love, family, friendship, home, work and finance have to offer?

Life is not always as it seems. Underlying issues, perception cause and effect, Karma, intention and soul purpose simultaneously play out together on levels unseen. For the seemingly miraculous to happen, for life to function properly, all aspects and all facets must work in sync – including us.

Life is not against you – it's working with you, providing daily what you ask for and what you need – though you may not realise. This is always the driving factor that drives life.

Deep within your psyche, within your own survival system, a higher sense of 'being' is creeping forward – you're part of something major going on – it's why you're here... Your own soul is ascending, a new world order is birthing through, you are evolving. *Divine Guidance* is written to help you recognise where you are within your journey and life agenda – so you can harness your personal power and regain control – regardless of what's unfolding in your now. Every time you use this book you'll get precisely what you need – without exception.

> *Divine Guidance* has the power to make a difference in your life; are you ready to use it?

> How truth can help you – I know well myself. Free of illusion and Ego – this book is a true inspiration that

will heighten your awareness and purpose to what is most needed – to inspire and help you move forward.

Deepak Chopra

Stephanie J. King is one of those rare people who seems to have a clear and continuous direct line to spirit. She works at a very high healing vibration and even in the time I have been involved with her much of my own baggage has simply fallen away. *Divine Guidance* will help you deepen your connection to Source and spontaneously bring in incredible clarity around even the most challenging situations.

Rachel Elnaugh, entrepreneur and star of BBV TV's Dragons' Den, now a Business Mentor and Transformational coach.

Grave Doubts
One Man's Incredible Afterlife Testimony – Death was never the option...

(I am I) What if you missed something important during the life you are currently living, something so fundamental and necessary that it would impact or hinder your soul's future progression? (I am I)

Simon was man's man. He believed in what could be seen, felt and measured, the beliefs that he carried, what he had learnt and the story he'd fought, loved and lived through. But was that correct or enough? One night, suddenly and without warning, he died... What he found he did not expect. No-one had forewarned or prepared him. Or did they, and would he have heard, understood or have listened?

Grave Doubts – is channelled from the next realm to encourage us to question, to question everything; to search further our beliefs and understanding of life, why we're here, what we're doing, aiming for and why; what makes us tick, why we live how we do and what our life efforts are for, what we take with us, why and what that in itself means to life now – just as much as to life moving forward when your time lived here is through.

Powerful information has been handed back across the ether, specifically channelled to help you – before it's too late and your own time spent here is over, to help your soul tick its own boxes; to make sense of what you've seen, been and lived through; to ensure fewer regrets of things you're unable to change...

Everything happens for a reason. Know precisely why things occurred or are happening – to crack the code that's been driving your own life...

Grave Doubts – will rock the core of deep-set held beliefs about life and death. Questions you carry – will be answered. If you've ever lost a loved one, this book will bring them safely back into your life when you know how close they are, why they're there and how they love you. If you're racked with grief, loss, pain and guilt, Grave Doubts will grant you understanding, healing and then peace. But most of all, this book will help you to be happy within THIS life, to help you grab it by the horns, see what you've created and make what you already have much better, as you wake up to truths of what's been happening...

You and your place in life are more significant than you know. No other book has been written like this before with such frank and open speaking. Are you ready to embark on the next phase of your life that's been standing / screaming / shouting to come in?

Don't miss this opportunity to grasp that...

Simon.

Believe & Achieve
The answers to teen success (especially great for adults too)

You are a living breathing work of art in a state of constant progress. You're creating and expressing even now as you read these words.

Nothing about you is haphazard. You choose your presentation, clothes, hair and makeup, the food you eat, music preferences, what you laugh and cry at, the books you read, TV programmes, films, hobbies and games you play, the type of friends you chill and mix with, how you spend your free time, conversation, sense of humour and more besides.

This book contains all you need to discover, to realise and understand your life's quest. But are you brave enough to give it a try?

Being a teen is the most important part of your development so far, yet it's often when you feel least acknowledged and understood. What would you like to change? What would it take for you to feel truly happy?

You have enormous potential; you can go anywhere and do all you wish. Love, security, happiness, abundance and success can be yours – much easier and faster than you think. In fact nothing need ever hold you back. But do you even know you are powerful – not powerless, and that life itself is willing you on?

You are part of the generation that will take life forward. Yours is the new wave of creativity and intellect. You see first-hand the world you'll inherit and you feel strongly about much that you deal with. Nothing is impossible. All options are open for you to explore and enjoy. This book will help you to finally BELIEVE in all you are and ACHIEVE all you are capable of and all you were born to be...

ACCESS YOUR HAPPINESS NOW

TRANSFORMATIONAL HOME WORKSHOP – delivered via email in bite size segments every 3rd day for 14 days (plus 2 extra bonus gifts).

Private – easy – powerful sessions – with a short '5' min film to watch and a couple of pages to read and then process. In 6 weeks or less you'll see and feel a new you emerge – completely in tune with your power; working and understanding life better; freed from baggage and hang ups of past.

This powerful, inspirational, informational – yet incredibly easy – set of video coaching sessions, mediations and exercises – is designed to free you of the confines of the past, lifting the lid of what unconsciously drives you to bring long lasting love to the fore and get life again working in tune with your needs; revealing a stronger, happier, healthier, more vibrant and confident you...

Know what holds you back; what and how you attract life; what has become your replacement for love... know what you need to feel loved and how you too love – friends, lovers, loved ones or self (sometimes the hardest love ever achieved)... Begin to see clearly what threads through your life to drive, overshadow, control you... We'll speak about Karma, reincarnation, ego, soul Agenda, Baggage and Patterns held on to or carried over...

Nothing will change until you start to change it – and this workshop shows you easily how!

Love, health, success and happiness are far easier to achieve than you think.

Available now from **www.stephaniejking.com**

'I Am' Meditations
Channelled Directly from Spirit

'I Am' is the first in a series of guided meditations unique in content and approach, allowing you to work directly with source – to bring in health, balance, harmony, understanding, forgiveness, love, light, peace, growth and extra sensory information – from the highest realms – to aid all. Because your own journey is unique, your needs, questions and inspirations will be also.

Before birth we each devised a real-time soul agenda, an overall life plan, with live tasks to set in motion, to recognise and work through. We have qualities to contribute, to overcome and accomplish, gifts that we alone can hone and harness to feed directly back to life as personal input, as our contribution and thanks for time spent here.

Many things are answered as you reassess your lot – with the aid of personal guides/your guardian/and with source. Physically, nothing is completely certain except we birth and die, yet far more occurs on levels unseen than we can ever imagine. The soul journey you are travelling is completely individual and unwritten – so what you will contribute, pay forward, or give back – is yours by personal choice and accomplishment.

Stephanie's works have been specifically channelled to help you work through Karma and what's occurring now – love, work, family, home – to highlight what lies hidden, to fine tune your highest attributes, strengths and gifts, and to help you to regain, to remember what has been lost.

(I am I) I will work with you – if you will work with me (I am I).

Internationally known and respected – Stephanie J. King – soulpreneur™ – has worked directly with the (I am I) consciousness and the higher spiritual/celestial realms for many decades – to re-awaken the soul; to channel guidance, inspiration, enlightenment, encouragement, self-empowerment and healing that's both powerful and applicable to all...

'I Am' Meditations - II
HIGHER STILL

'I am' Meditations are the perfect solution to inner wisdom, higher guidance, clarity and focus for the busy lives we lead. Information is always available – for the Universe knows what we need and what is lacking; our soul agenda and potential; so it's natural that we're supported as our real-time living story continues to unfold...

HIGHER STILL the second in a series of powerful guided mediations, is even stronger in channelled energy, for what was given in live recording will flow to you directly – to bring in health, abundance, balance, harmony, understanding, forgiveness, love, light, peace, growth and extra sensory information – in tune with where you are, from higher realms.

Before birth we each devised a real-time soul agenda, an overall plan that now plays out. What we don't complete in this life will go forward with us to the next as earthly baggage, to again become our Karma later on.

We have an opportunity to make a difference, to make life work. We are ascending. Life and energy are speeding up to assist us with this process. The time to make adjustments is right now.

Stephanie's works have been specifically channelled to help you work through what's occurring now – in matters of love, work, family, home – to highlight what lies hidden, to fine tune higher strengths, to help you to remember and regain what you have lost...

(I am I) I will work with you – if you will work with Me.
(I Am I)

In these meditations you'll actually hear Stephanie's speaking voice change as the higher realms speak through her and use her voice... All energies received during live recording - will now directly flow to you – as nothing has been altered or removed... They're very powerful...

'Believe & Achieve' Meditations

Increase intuition and awareness
Perfect for teens and the inner child in adults.

Being a teen is the most important part of your development so far, yet it's often when you feel the least acknowledged and understood... Where you feel most pushed and pummelled by life and others...

What would you like to change? What do you need to function better? What would it take for you to feel happy, acknowledged and accepted – for who you are?

You have enormous potential; you can go anywhere and do all things you wish. Love, security, happiness, abundance, confidence and success can be yours – much easier and faster than you think. In fact nothing need ever hold you back. But do you even know that you are truly powerful – not powerless, and that you are an important cog within the workings of this 'now' time playing out, and that life itself is constantly spurring you on?

You are part of the generation that will take life forward. Yours is the new wave of creativity and intellect birthing through. You see first-hand the world that you'll inherit and you feel strongly about much you have to deal with. Yet nothing is impossible. All options are open for you to explore, fine tune, reshape, invent and enjoy.

These special, guided meditations were downloaded to precisely help you understand you own power and potential. Very quickly you'll find yourself more focused, relaxed and open to new ideas flowing in, and because you'll stress and experience anger less, relationships on all levels will feel the benefit. The brilliance of who you are will be apparent for all to see. Life will flow far easier in the directions you most want – and you'll be happy...

ARE YOU READY?

Stephanie's works have been specifically channelled to help you work through Karma and what's occurring now – to propel you forward, to help you grow and recognise your highest strengths, gifts, attributes and personal talents; to help you to enjoy the life you live...

Internationally known and respected Stephanie J. King – Soulpreneur™ - works with the 'I am I' consciousness and the higher realms to reawaken each soul to its reason for being... to channel guidance, inspiration, enlightenment, encouragement, self-empowerment, confidence, understanding, love and healing – that's powerful, necessary; up-to-the-minute and applicable to all...

Again - are you ready to explore this?

For further information - to keep abreast of appearances, new releases and magazine, blog entries –
visit **www.stephaniejking.com**

NOTES

NOTES

NOTES

9 781913 192334